K
Ladakh &
Zanskar

Kashmir, Ladakh & Zanskar

Published by:
Lonely Planet Publications
PO Box 88, South Yarra
Victoria 3141, Australia

Printed by:
Colorcraft, Hong Kong

Typeset by:
Lonely Planet Publications

Designed by:
Andrena Millen

Photographs by:
colour: 129 BC, 161 BC Rolf Schettler, others Tony Wheeler
black & white: 140 Maureen Wheeler, others Rolf Schettler

Translated by:
Neil Kirk

First Published
February 1981

Schettler, Rolf.
[Kaschmir und Ladakh. English].
Kashmir, Ladakh & Zanskar.

Additional information by Tony Wheeler.
ISBN 0 908086 21 0.

1. Kashmir — Description and travel — Guide-books.
1. Schettler, Margret. II. Wheeler, Anthony Ian,
1946-. III. Kirk, Neil. IV. Title.

915.4'604

Lonely Planet Guides

Across Asia on the Cheap
Africa on the Cheap
Australia — a travel survival kit
Burma — a travel survival kit
Europe — a travel survival kit*
Hong Kong, Macau & Canton
Israel & the Occupied Territories
Kashmir, Ladakh & Zanskar
Kathmandu & the Kingdom
* of Nepal*
New Zealand — a travel survival kit
Papua New Guinea — a travel
* survival kit*
The Philippines — a travel
* survival kit*
South America on a Shoestring
South-East Asia on a Shoestring
Sri Lanka — a travel survival kit
Trekking in the Himalayas
USA West

* this book is available only in Australasia

Lonely Planet travel guides are available around the world. If you can't find them, ask your bookshop to order them from one of the distributors listed below. For countries not listed or if you would like a free copy of our latest booklist write to Lonely Planet in Australia.

Australia — Lonely Planet Publications Pty Ltd, PO Box 88, South Yarra, Victoria 3141.
Canada — Milestone Publications, Box 6006, Victoria, British Columbia, V8P 5L4.
Hong Kong — The Book Society, GPO Box 7804, Hong Kong.
India — UBS Distributors, 5 Ansari Rd, New Delhi, 110002.
Japan — Intercontinental Marketing Corp, IPO Box 5056, Tokyo 100-31.
Malaysia — see Singapore
Nepal — see India
Netherlands — Nilsson & Lamm bv, Post bus 195, Pampuslaan 212, 1680 AD Weesp.
New Zealand — Caveman Press, PO Box 1458, Dunedin.
Papua New Guinea — Gordon & Gotch (PNG), PO Box 3395, Port Moresby.
Philippines — see Singapore
Singapore — Apa Productions, 349 Pasir Panjang Rd, Singapore, 0511.
Thailand — Chalermnit, 1-2 Erawan Arcade, Bangkok.
UK — Roger Lascelles, 16 Holland Park Gardens, London, W14 8DY.
USA (West) — Bookpeople, 2940 Seventh St, Berkeley, CA 94710.
USA (East) — Hippocrene Books, 171 Madison Ave, New York, NY 10016.
West Germany — Versandhaus Sud-West, PO Box 3680, D-7900 Ulm.
                   — Buchvertrieb Gerda Schettler, Postfach 64, D-3415 Hattorf a H.

Rolf and Margret Schettler were, in 1974, the first foreign visitors to Ladakh with their own vehicle. They have subsequently returned to Ladakh and to Zanskar to write about, film and record the music of these remote Himalayan regions. This book was first published in Germany as *Kaschmir & Ladakh* and expanded, at the same time as this English language edition, to include Zanskar.

Thanks from the Author
To Sheikh Maqbul Ahmad and Nazeer Ahmad Butt, to D N Dhar, Shri Mehmood-ur-Rehman, Mohamad Ashraf, M Asaf Mahmud, A Hakim, Akbar Ladakhi, A A Wani, M Aslam Lingrou, Sonam Khangsar, Iqbal Chapri, Phunchok Wangtak, the Rani of Stok and many other Ladakhis, particularly the people of Mulbekh and Leh.

And this English Edition
We visited Kashmir and Ladakh prior to the publication of this English language edition and added some new material on the Vale of Kashmir and the area of Ladakh around Leh. We would also like to thank our friend of many years Ashok Khanna (who flew to Ladakh with us but wasn't on the flight when we finally managed to land), Angus Lindsay (who was), Michael Wall and Lizzie Slater, David Stanley (and other people who have written with useful information) and, most important, Iqbal of the houseboats Bambari Palace, New Lucky Kashmir, Lorrine and London House. Without him I don't think we would even have got on the (heavily overbooked) flight to Leh. Nice houseboats too!

Tony & Maureen Wheeler

Contents

Introduction

Kashmir, Ladakh and Zanskar are all regions of the Indian state of Jammu and Kashmir, often referred to simply as J&K. Jammu is the southern part of the state and forms a transitional area between the Indian plains and the mighty Himalayas. Correctly the rest of the state is Kashmir but in practice the title is reserved for the 'Vale of Kashmir', a large Himalayan valley in the north of the state. Ladakh and Zanskar are regions of Kashmir, geographical neighbours to Kashmir proper but separated from Kashmir by the full height of the Himalayas and worlds away in terms of people, culture and religion. Parts of Kashmir are under Pakistani control, principally the Gilgit and Hunza areas, and the Chinese hold a slice of Ladakh to the east. Although the whole Kashmir region is a subject of considerable dispute, particularly between India and Pakistan, the continuing argument is highly unlikely to have any effect on foreign visitiors.

Jammu is not of great interest to most overseas visitors to the region, it's basically just a stop-over on the trip up to Srinagar. As well as being a geographical transition zone from the hot plains to the cool mountains, it is also a religious change-point. Here the Hindu religion begins to give way to the Moslem religion that predominates in the Kashmir Valley. The Vale of Kashmir has been famous for its great natural beauty ever since the days of the Moghul emperors. The great Moghuls further embellished that natural beauty with a series of delightfully planned gardens, many of which are still beautifully preserved even today. The British added a further attraction to Kashmir, the houseboats which crowd Dal Lake at Srinagar — no visit to Kashmir is complete without a stay on a houseboat.

Ladakh lies across the Himalayas from Kashmir — its situation on the Tibetan plateau plus the clear Tibetan influence in the Ladakhi's customs and religion has led to it being known as 'little Tibet'. Ladakh's quite incredibly barren landscape, a result of the high Himalayan barrier which prevents rain clouds from climbing across from the lush valleys to the south and west, has also given it the name of 'the moonland'. Ladakh has only been open to tourists since the mid-70s and until 1962, when the Chinese invasion prompted the rapid construction of a road linking Ladakh with Srinagar, getting into Ladakh involved several weeks hard walk. Since 1979 you can actually fly to Ladakh, in less than 30 minutes from Srinagar.

Finally there is Zanskar, a long valley running in a roughly north-west to south-east direction between Kashmir and Ladakh. The people are much like the Ladakhis in their dress, customs and religion but they have been even more isolated from outside contact. Like Ladakh, visitors have only been allowed into Zanskar in the last few years but access to Zanskar is much more difficult. A jeep track to Padum, the Zanskar 'capital', will only be completed during the early '80s and most visitors to Zanskar will continue to arrive on foot or by pony. The whole Kashmir, Ladakh and Zanskar

Tikse Gompa
near Leh, Ladakh

region is a paradise for trekkers with trails leading through beautiful and spectacular scenery, far from the encroachment of modern roads and motor vehicles.

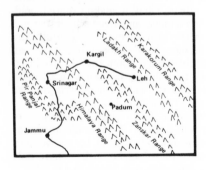

GEOGRAPHY

The Himalayan range runs roughly north-west to south-east through the state of Jammu & Kashmir. The Himalayas separate the Vale of Kashmir from the Zanskar Valley and in turn Zanskar is separated from Ladakh by the Zanskar Range. The Kashmir Valley is bounded to the south-west by the lower Pir Panjal Range. At one time Kashmir was a lake which, like the Kathmandu Valley, was drained eons ago.

FACTS

The state of Jammu and Kashmir has an area of 222,236 square km and a population of about four million. Ladakh, with an area of just under 100,000 square km, comprises nearly half of the whole state making it the largest district in India. However its population of just over 100,000 also makes it the most lightly populated region of India.

VISAS

If you're from Australia, New Zealand, Great Britain, Canada or Ireland you're in luck, no visas are needed and you can stay in India almost indefinitely. India's historic tolerance extends to those tourists who do not require visas — they can wander around India forever. If you're from West Germany or the Scandinavian countries you can stay for up to 90 days without a visa.

Most other nationalities require a visa for visiting India. They're issued at Indian embassies and are valid for 90 days and can be extended for a further 90 days. Indian visas are usually triple entry so you can exit to Nepal or Sri Lanka and return on the same visa. Note that extending an Indian visa is usually such a complicated, bureaucratic hassle that it is advisable, if you leave India to a neighbouring country, to get a new visa and start your 90 days again.

With your visa you will also get a Tourist Introduction Card, the main purpose of which is that it serves as a permit to buy alcohol in 'dry' areas. Some Indian states still practise prohibition. If you do not need a visa you can get a Tourist Introduction Card simply by asking for one at an Indian tourist office. Note that there is no prohibition in Jammu and Kashmir except for certain 'dry days'.

You no longer require special permits for visiting Kashmir or Ladakh although it is advisable to enquire about permits before setting off on trekking trips, particularly into Zanskar. Some places in Ladakh and Zanskar are only accessible with special permission which may have to be obtained in New Delhi. The area of Ladakh from one mile north of the Srinagar-Leh road is a 'restricted zone' and completely banned to foreigners. The same restriction applies to the area from one mile east of the Leh-Manali road although it is extremely difficult, if not impossible, to get permission to travel along this military road at all.

MONEY

US$1	=	7.8 rupees
A$1	=	8.9 rupees
£1	=	17.8 rupees

There are 100 paise (p) to the rupee (Rs). At one time the rupee was divided up into 16 annas and you may still find prices quoted in annas in bazaars and markets — four annas is 25p, eight annas is 50p. There is no longer any blackmarket to speak of in India and it is illegal to import or export Indian currency although you can generally get Indian rupees in Bangkok or Singapore or in Europe at a useful discount. You are allowed to bring a bottle of whisky and a carton of cigarettes into India duty free and these are usually an excellent investment.

The major travellers' cheques are all easily exchanged in India although US dollars and pounds sterling are the most readily recognised foreign currencies. In out-of-the-way centres you may find these are the only currencies readily accepted. Anything to do with paperwork in India is inevitably time consuming so you may find it easier to change larger sums at one time than you would in other countries — simply in order to minimise the time wasted in banks.

Try not to have money transferred to you in India, it is painfully slow and laborious, particularly with the Indian banks. If you must have funds sent to India transfer them by cable or telex, not by mail, even if you have plenty of time in hand, and transfer them to a foreign owned bank. American Express have offices in Bombay, New Delhi and Calcutta but there are other banks operating throughout India which are still foreign owned and are much more efficient than the Indian owned banks, particularly when it comes to foreign transactions. The Chartered Bank and Grindlays Bank are two examples — Grindlays have an office in Srinagar on the Bund.

There are two particular points to be careful about with Indian money. First avoid dirty, grubby or torn notes — they can be unusable, particularly in out-of-the-way places. If you do get stuck with such a note try not to worry about it or cause any hassle if people refuse to accept it. You can easily get them changed at a bank or use them for some official purpose such as paying your airport departure tax. The other money problem is big notes — changing a Rs 100 banknote is always difficult, in fact with India's perpetual small change deficiency changing anything is usually difficult. When changing foreign currency at a bank try to get as much of it in smaller denomination notes as possible. This problem applies particularly in Ladakh where during the summer, tourist, season there is a severe shortage of small denomination notes — bring as many one and two rupee notes as possible. Note that in Zanskar there are no facilities for changing money, nor in Ladakh outside of Leh or Kargil. Make sure that you have enough rupees with you.

CLIMATE
The climatic differences in the state of Jammu and Kashmir are probably the most varied in all of India — in Jammu in the hot season the temperatures can be consistently above 40°C while at Kargil in mid-winter the temperature has been known to drop to -40°C, a temperature differential of 150°F! Similarly Jammu, during the monsoon, can have rain every day while in Ladakh whole years may pass with no rainfall at all. Briefly the weather you can expect in the various regions is detailed below:

Jammu Situated at a height of only 300 metres, Jammu has the three-season weather typical of the Indian plains. The best time of year in Jammu is the cool season from early October to about February-March. In October, immediately after the monsoon finishes, the weather will be cool and fresh, the skies clear and dust free. Later in the cool season (December and January in particular) it can get quite crisp with temperatures as low as 5°C at night. In February-March the temperature starts to climb as you enter the hot season. By April, May and June it gets uncomfortably hot and dry. Since there has been no rain for some time the air is very dusty and the temperature scarcely seems to drop at night. Towards the end of the hot season the mercury will sit at 40°C or above for days on end. Finally the monsoon arrives around the beginning of July; the dust is immediately cleared out of the air although for some time the temperature change is merely from hot and dry to hot and sticky.

Kashmir At an altitude of over 1000 metres the Kashmir Valley is much cooler than Jammu and it is at its most popular in May-June when Indian tourists flood up from the hot, airless plains. At this time the daily temperatures are around 20°C, a delightfully cool contrast to the 40°C temperatures common on the plains to the south. In July and August it can get rather hotter and the valley somewhat humid and still — the simple solution is to move out to one of the smaller resorts that lie around the valley rim. At places like Pahalgam, Gulmarg and Sonamarg the altitude ensures cooler weather even in mid-summer. The Kashmir tourist season ends in October as minimum temperatures drop down below 10°C and from November to February night time temperatures often fall below freezing in Srinagar, snow falls and during cold years Dal Lake can actually freeze over. In the winter Gulmarg becomes India's number one ski-resort. Rainfall in Kashmir is fairly even year round.

Ladakh & Zanskar Winter at the high altitudes of Ladakh and Zanskar can be spectacularly cold although snow fall is generally not heavy since the Himalayas act as a barrier to rain clouds coming up from the south. Temperatures are consistently below freezing for six months of the year in Leh and the snowbound pass into Kashmir isolates Ladakh from October to June. Drass is reputed to be one of the coldest places in Asia during the winter. In summer the day time temperatures are pleasantly warm, maximums around 20 to 25°C but night time temperatures are always crisp. Even at the height of summer the temperature will immediately plummet when a cloud obscures the sun. You should always have a sweater handy in Ladakh. Beware of the power of the sun at this altitude, you will quickly get a bad case of sunburn even on a cool day.

The chart below details the average maximum temperature ($^{\circ}$C), average minimum temperature ($^{\circ}$C) and average monthly rainfall (mm) in New Delhi, Srinagar and Leh:

	New Delhi*			Srinagar**			Leh***		
	max	min	rain	max	min	rain	max	min	rain
January	21.1	6.7	22.9	5.0	-2.2	73.7	-1.1	-13.3	10.2
February	23.9	9.4	17.7	7.2	-1.1	71.1	0.6	-12.2	7.6
March	30.6	14.4	12.7	13.9	3.3	91.4	7.2	-6.1	7.6
April	36.1	20.0	7.7	18.9	7.2	93.9	13.3	-1.1	5.0
May	40.6	26.1	12.7	24.4	11.1	60.9	16.1	0.6	5.0
June	38.9	28.3	73.7	29.4	14.4	35.6	20.0	6.7	5.0
July	35.6	27.2	180.3	31.1	18.3	58.4	25.0	10.0	12.9
August	33.9	26.1	172.7	30.6	17.8	60.9	23.9	10.0	15.2
September	33.9	23.9	116.8	27.8	12.2	38.1	21.1	5.6	7.6
October	33.9	18.3	10.2	22.2	5.0	30.5	15.0	-0.6	2.5
November	28.9	11.1	2.5	15.6	-0.6	10.2	8.3	-6.7	2.5
December	22.8	7.8	10.2	10.7	-2.2	33.0	2.2	-10.6	5.0
annual rainfall			640.2			657.7			83.8

*1866-1943
**1899-1942
***1881-1942

HEALTH & IMMUNISATIONS
There are a number of immunisations which you are either recommended or required to have. These can be provided by your own doctor or health service and should then be entered on your International Certificate of Vaccination. Smallpox, which is valid for three years, and cholera, valid for six months, are the two most important immunisations. Gamma Globulin as protections against hepatitis is of questionable efficacy although an improved version has recently been introduced. Your doctor may also recommend that you be immunised against typhoid-paratyphoid, tetanus and polio.

Although malarial mosquitos are not exactly at home in Ladakh and Zanskar, India as a whole is an area of malarial risk, even in New Delhi and you should take anti-malarial tablets, either the daily or weekly variety. Other medicine you should bring include lomotil or other anti-diarrhoeals but remember the best treatment for mild diarrhoea is to let your own system fight it off. If you're planning to trek in Ladakh and Zanskar bring sleeping pills and aspirin since sleeplessness and headaches are two common afflictions when trekking at high altitudes. In Srinagar you will find a wide variety of medicines readily available and without the prescriptions normally required in the west.

For comprehensive information on health while travelling see *The Traveller's Health Guide* by Dr Anthony C Turner (Roger Lascelles, London, 1979) — it's available from Lonely Planet.

TREKKING IN KASHMIR, LADAKH OR ZANSKAR

Trekking in the Indian Himalayas is still a very low-key activity compared to Nepal where there are now a large number of trekking agencies and organisers. There are also a number of ground rules that make trekking in Kashmir a rather different proposition to trekking in Nepal. For a general introduction to Himalayan trekking get a copy of *Trekking in the Himalayas* by Stan Armington, available from Lonely Planet.

The major difference between Nepalese and Indian trekking is a factor of the smaller number of trekkers. Srinagar does not have the large number of trekking agencies which you find in Kathmandu. Therefore there are not the many organised treks that operate in Nepal. If you do wish to explore Kashmir on an organised trek one of the most experienced operators in the Kashmir Himalayas is Australian-Himalayan Expeditions, 3rd floor, 28-34 O'Connell St, Sydney 2000, Australia.

For similar reasons you cannot so easily rent or buy equipment in Srinagar whereas in Kathmandu there are many shops with everything from boots, packs and parkas to tents and sleeping bags available for purchase or hire. In Kashmir you must come fully equipped. Another major difference from Nepal to Kashmir is porters — they are not so readily found as in Nepal and they are more expensive, more so in Kashmir compared to Zanskar or Ladakh. Pack ponies are, however, widely used in Kashmir and can be hired from any of the main hill stations.

Trekking is not Climbing   Don't confuse trekking with mountaineering. Although you may reach considerable heights, trekking basically means following the walking tracks used by local people in places where there are no vehicle roads.

Physical Requirements   You should be in reasonably good physical condition, particularly for the high altitudes you may encounter. Trekking involves a lot of up and down walking.

Equipment   You need good walking shoes, warm clothing (down gear for very high altitudes), a good quality sleeping bag, a comfortable pack, sunglasses, food, medical equipment. Detailed suggestions on the selection of trekking equipment are made in *Trekking in the Himalayas.*

Food   In Kashmir, and more particularly in Zanskar and Ladakh, you will not usually be able to obtain food along the trekking routes — you must carry adequate supplies with you. Srinagar is the best place to do your pre-trek outfitting. Although supplies are also available in Kargil and Leh, and to a lesser extent in Padum, the choice will be much less and costs much higher. Tinned or packaged food suitable for carrying on treks is generally rather more expensive in India than in the west. In Ladakh and Zanskar the extreme lack of vegetation means it is often impossible to cook on a fire —

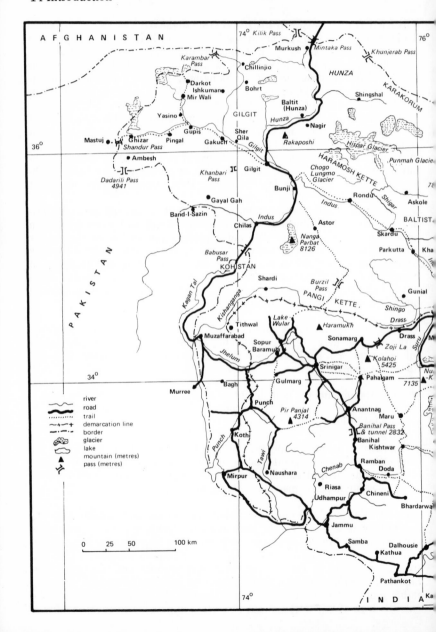

Kashmir, Ladakh & Zanskar

C H I N A

78° 80°

36°

Aghil Depsang Pass

in K2 Muztagh K5

Golden Throne Karakorum Pass Haijilanjia

Siachen Glacier 5575 Sumnal 6433 Khitai Davan Pass 5341

Rimo Muztagh

Chulung Group 6620 Nubra Qizyl Jilga Thaldat

hyok Changlung AKSAI CHIN

ADAKH Panamik Sumdo

Shyok Under Chinese Control

LADAKH Samzungling

Khalsi Nia La Chang Lung La 5764 Nischu

La Khardung La 5602 Shamal Lungpa

Lamayuru Nimmu Chang Chenmo Lanak La 5486

mika La Alchi Shyok Pamzal Kyam

Shishi La Leh Tikse Shey Tankse Niagzu

Singi La Stok KETE Kyaugang La 5472

La Hemis Gompa Upshi Mun 34°

La Khurna Chang La 5368 Pangong Tso

Zanskar Miru Taglang La

KAR Zangla Rezang La

Karsha Gompa Tsaka La 4724

Padum Thonde Rukchen C H I N A

Marang La Thangra (Tibet)

was Char RUPSHU Indus

Kargiakh Sutak Karzok Hanle

ch Shingo La 5097 Lake Tso Morari Hanle Tara La

Triloknath Bara Lacha La 4891 Demchok Tashigong

Darcha LAHUL & SPITI 80°

Tandi Keylong Losar Charding La Pass

Ravi Rohtang Pass Khoksar 78°

Manali Parachu

ramsala Hamta Jot Pass 3477

Baijnath Kulu

you need a kerosene stove and kerosene in a strong, leakproof container. Remember that the high altitudes in Zanskar and Ladakh result in a much lower boiling point for water — a pressure cooker is very useful.

Accommodation Although a tent can be very useful there are many government rest houses or dak bungalows along trekking routes — more so in Kashmir than in Zanskar or Ladakh. You can also sometimes find shelter in tea houses or peoples' homes. Generally this sort of accommodation, as in the gompas of Zanskar and Ladakh, will consist of little more than a bare room.

Routes & Maps Some of the main treks are described in the relative sections on Kashmir, Ladakh and Zanskar. Note that many of these treks go from one region into the next — from Zanskar to Ladakh or Kashmir to Zanskar for example. Good trekking maps are virtually impossible to obtain in Kashmir. The J&K Tourist Office has only a very poor quality aerial photograph map with no routes marked on it. The Lhasa Restaurant in Srinagar sells a good quality French map of Zanskar and Ladakh. A problem with any map or other information on trekking in this area is the widely varying ways of spelling place names. This book is undoubtedly no exception although it tries

making butter tea
in Lamayuru Gompa

to follow the most commonly used variations. The J&K Tourist Office has a small brochure titled *Trekking in Jammu & Kashmir* which may provide some useful information.

Permission Although there is no system of trekking permits, as required in Nepal, there are limitations on where you may trek. In particular you are constrained by the security zone requirements that you do not go more than a mile north of the Zoji La-Kargil-Leh road and the similar restriction along the Leh-Manali road. This limits Zanskar and Ladakh trekking to the Suru, Zanskar and Kishtwar valleys. For trekking in other areas permission must be obtained from the Ministry of Home Affairs, Government of India, New Delhi.

Snow Bridges These are a particular hazard of Kashmiri trekking, especially during the spring-summer melt. In many places rivers are completely covered by snow and ice during the winter, while the rivers continue to flow underneath. During the thaw this cover often melts to isolated 'bridges' which trekkers can sometimes cross. Take care, if you fall through a snowbridge the drop may be less than a metre and only result in wet feet but it can be a long, fatal fall. There are certain well known snow bridges which appear every year.

Health & Medicine If you're going on an organised trek the trek organisers will supply you with a list of the necessary immunisations and will probably require that you complete a medical examination before departing. See the introductory section on health for general information about health and immunisations. Maintaining your health while trekking is principally a matter of taking care in what you eat and drink. Always ensure that drinking water has been boiled or sterilised.

GENERAL INFORMATION

Time
India is 5½ hours ahead of GMT, 4½ hours behind Australian Eastern Standard Time, 10½ hours ahead of American Eastern Standard Time.

Business Hours
Shops and offices are generally open from 10 am to 5 pm, they're late starters! Banks are open 10 am to 2 pm on weekdays, 10 am to noon on Saturdays. Post offices are open 10 am to 5 pm on weekdays and also on Saturday mornings.

Electricity
230-240 volts, 50 cycles, alternating current — breakdowns and blackouts are not unusual. In Leh electricity only operates in the evenings.

Film

Colour film is difficult to find in India and expensive. Most colour film you do see on sale has been sold to the shops by tourists. If you're planning to take photographs bring plenty of film with you, Kashmir and Ladakh are very photogenic. In Ladakh remember to allow for the extreme intensity of the light at this altitude.

Books & Bookshops

India has many surprisingly good bookshops, particularly in New Delhi. There are several bookshops in Srinagar which usually have the latest books of local interest. There are a number of locally published guidebooks to Kashmir. There are many older books on Kashmir and Ladakh worth searching out in libraries and there are also a number of recently published coffee-table books on these picturesque regions.

The Japanese 'This Beautiful World Series' of illustrated paperbacks published by Kodansha International includes a book on *Kashmir. Freedom at Midnight* by Larry Collins and Dominique Lapierre, that highly readable book on India's rocky path to independence, has an interesting description of the stormy events in Kashmir at that time. It's available in India in a low price Bell Books/Vikas Publishing paperback.

National Geographic had a feature on Ladakh in the March 1978 issue. *Zanskar — The Hidden Kingdom* by Michel Peissel (Collins & Harvill Press, London, 1979) is an interesting account of a trek through Zanskar shortly after it was reopened to foreign tourists. For a thorough introduction to Himalayan trekking see *Trekking in the Himalayas* by Stan Armington (Lonely Planet, Melbourne, 1979).

Seven Years in Tibet by Heinrich Harrer is a best-selling account of the author's adventures in Tibet before the Chinese occupation. *Tibet* by Thubten Jigme Norbu and Colin Turnbull is an excellent account of the culture and religion of Tibet, co-authored by the brother of the Dalai Lama.

Newspapers & Media

The major English language Indian papers arrive in Srinagar daily. You'll also find *Time, Newsweek* and India's own excellent news-magazine *India Today* on Srinagar's news-stands. Srinagar has its own TV channel.

LANGUAGE

Although English is widely spoken in Kashmir it never hurts to know a little of the local language. Indians speak a vast number of regional languages including, in the state of Jammu and Kashmir, Kashmiri, Ladakhi and Urdu. But Hindi is the official 'national' language and widely spoken. Some useful words:

where is a hotel (tourist office)?	hotal (turist afis) kahan hai?
how far is ....?	.........kitni dur hai?

what is your name?			apka shubh nam?
how do I get to		.... kojane ke liye kaise jana parega?	

hello, goodbye	namaste	what is your name?	
yes/no	han/nahin		apka shubh nam?
please	meharbani se	what is the time?	
thank you	shukriya, dhanyawad		kya baja hai?
how much?	kitne paise?	come here	yahan ao
this is expensive		show me the menu	
	yeh bahut mehnga hai		mujha minu dikhao
		the bill please	bill lao

big	bara	night	rat
today	tambaku	week	saptah
day	din	month	mahina
		year	sal

medicine	dawa	rice	inam
ice	baraf	tea	chai
egg	anda	coffee	kafi
fruit	phal	milk	dudh
vegetable	sabzi	sugar	chini
		butter	makkhan

1	ek	6	chhe
2	do	7	sat
3	tin	8	ath
4	char	9	nau
5	panch	10	das

100	sau
100,000	lakh
10,000,000	crore

INFORMATION

Government of India Tourist offices overseas include:

Australia	Carlton Centre, 55 Elizabeth St, Sydney, NSW 2000 (tel 02 232 1600)
	Elder House, 111 St George's Terrace, Perth, WA 6000 (tel 06 321 6932)
Canada	Suite 1016, Royal Trust Tower (PO Box 342), Toronto Dominion Centre, Toronto 1, Ontario (tel 416 362 3188)
Japan	Pearl building, 9-18 Ginza, 7 Chome, Chuo ku, Tokyo (tel 571 5062/3)

Singapore	Podium Block, 4th floor, Ming Court Hotel, Tanglin Rd, Singapore 10 (tel 235 5737)
Sweden	Sveavagen 9-11 (Box 40016), 103-41 Stockholm 40 (tel 08 215081)
Thailand	Singapore Airlines Building, 3rd floor, 62/5 Thaniya Rd, Bangkok
UK	21 New Bond St, London W1Y ODY (tel 01 493 0769)
USA	30 Rockefeller Plaza, 15 North Mezzanine, New York, NY 10020 (tel 212 586 4901) 201 North Michigan Ave, Chicago, Illinois 60601 (tel 312 236 6899) 3550 Wilshire Blvd, Suite 204, Los Angeles, California 90010 (tel 213 380 8855)

In India Government of India Tourist Offices you may find useful include:

Bombay	123 M Karve Rd (tel 293144)
Calcutta	4 Shakespeare Sarani (tel 441402)
Madras	35 Mount Rd (tel 86240)
New Delhi	88 Janpath (tel 320005)

In Jammu and Kashmir itself there are J&K Tourist Offices at:

| Jammu | Tourist Reception Centre, Vir Marg (tel 5324) |
| Srinagar | Tourist Reception Centre (tel 2449, 3648, 2927 & 6209) |

The J&K Tourist Department also has smaller offices in Pahalgam, in Leh and in Padum. Elsewhere there are Kashmir Government Tourist Offices at:

Ahmedabad	Airlines House, Lal Darwaza (tel 20473)
Bombay	Manekji Wadia Building, 129 Mahatma Gandhi Rd (tel 273830)
Calcutta	Kashmir Government Arts Emporium, 12 Chow- ringhee (tel 233268)
New Delhi	Chandralok Building, 36 Janpath (tel 345373)
Pathankot	Railway Station (tel 57)

Getting to India

From Europe The official fare from London to Bombay or New Delhi is £426 economy one-way, £540 for a 90-day excursion (round trip ticket) or £466 for a 120-day excursion. In actual fact you can find one-way tickets at less than £200 — check the travel page ads in *The Times* or *Time Out*. It's still possible to overland to India, troubles in Iran and Afghanistan or not. The overland companies take the southern route through Iran, dipping down to Isfahan, crossing the desert to Zahedan then entering Pakistan to Quetta. This route avoids Afghanistan completely. It's also possible to make the trip by public transport and recent visitors to Iran report that it's relatively friendly, prices are more competitive and travel is no problem — so long as you're not American! For full details see *Across Asia on the Cheap* from Lonely Planet Publications.

From the USA Air fares from the USA are more complex than anywhere else in the world so it's wise to see a travel agent for the latest information. One-way advance purchase fares from New York start from around US$650. Round trip excursion fares start from around US$1060. From the west coast it may be worth looking into cheap fares to south-east Asia and then flying on from there.

From Australia India's out in the cold when it comes to cheap fares from Oz. There are advance purchase (Apex) tickets to South-East Asia and to Europe — but not to India, in between the two regions. Until Apex fares are introduced for India the fare to Bombay or Delhi from Sydney or Melbourne is A$864 one-way. There is an excursion round trip fare at A$998 but it only permits a maximum stay of 60 days.
   There are several possible alternatives: One is to simply shop around, travel agents still indulge in price cutting! Another is to fly with Student Travel (if you're a 'student'). They have one-way and return fares to Calcutta for A$475/865 and Delhi for A$571/930 with no maximum-minimum stay requirements. Or you could take an Apex ticket to Singapore or Bangkok and fly on from there. One-way to Singapore is A$358/456 off peak/peak and to Bangkok it's A$467/544. So long as the fares to India remain so out of line with those to South-East Asia this will be a cheaper way than flying direct. Return Apex fares are A$512 to 700 to Singapre, A$610 to 835 to Bangkok. For full details on 'overlanding' from Australia, through South-East Asia to India see *South-East Asia on a Shoestring*.

From South-East Asia Singapore and Bangkok are the two cheap air fare centres of the region. From Singapore you can fly to Madras for S$500 (US$235) or to Bombay for S$650 (US$305). From Bangkok it costs about 2000 baht (US$100) to fly to Calcutta or 3000 baht (US$150) to fly to

New Delhi. You can also take the regular shipping service from Penang in Malaysia to Madras, but this is no financial saving over flying.

Returning from India New Delhi is the best place to look for cheap flights out of India. Delhi to Australia will cost around Rs 5500, Delhi-Europe from Rs 3500 to Rs 4000 depending on the carrier. One of the best places to go for ticket information in Delhi is the Student Travel Information Centre (STIC) at the Hotel Imperial, Janpath, New Delhi (tel 344789, 345938 and 344965).

Jammu

Jammu, the second largest town in the state of Jammu and Kashmir, has a population of about 160,000. It's situated 580 km from Delhi and 290 km from Srinagar on the south-eastern slopes of the Siwalik range. In winter it becomes the headquarters of the J&K administration and many Kashmiris move here for the winter because the temperature does not drop below 5°C. Due to its low altitude (300 metres) the summers can get uncomfortably hot (over 40°C) and the humid, unpleasant conditions also bring on plagues of gnats.

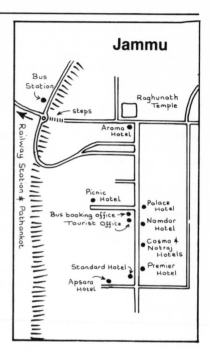

For those interested in languages one can hear Hindi, Kashmiri, English, Urdu, Punjabi and Dogra spoken in Jammu. Although Jammu has been dubbed 'the city of temples' it is not of particular interest to tourists; most travellers tend to use it only as an overnight stop on the way to or from Kashmir. Unless you fly you will almost certainly pass through Jammu.

Although legends tell of the city being founded by a Raja Jamboo Loochen thousands of years ago, there is no positive historical record prior to the 18th century. In 1832 the states of Jammu and Kashmir were merged and they continued under the rule of the Dogras until India's independence.

The old city of Jammu is perched on a hilltop beside the Tawi River. A new town sprawls away from the hillside and extends for some distance across the other side of the river. Principal places of interest in Jammu include:

Raghunath Temple

Situated in the centre of the city, only a short stroll from the Tourist Reception Centre, this is the largest temple complex in northern India. Construction of the temple started in 1835, under Maharaja Gulab Singh, the founder of the present city of Jammu. The Purani Mandi, like the main complex dedicated to Lord Rama, was built in 1888 by Maharaja Ranbir Singh's wife. The smaller temples surrounding the courtyard are dedicated to various gods and goddesses who feature in the Ramayana.

Rambireswar Temple

Also centrally located, this Shiva temple was built in 1883 by Maharaja Ranbir Singh and features a number of crystal Shiva lingams and the tallest shikara in the city.

Dogra Art Gallery

The collection here includes over 500 paintings of the Basohli, Jammu and Kangra schools. The Basohli-style miniature paintings here are of particular importance and interest. The gallery also houses a collection of sculptures, terracotta pieces, murals, weapons and illustrated manuscripts. The gallery is situated in the Gandhi Bhavan by the New Secretariat. It is open from 7.30 am to 1 pm in summer and from 11 am to 5 pm in winter except on Mondays when it is closed. Admission is free.

Bahu Fort

Clinging to a rock face on the opposite bank of the Tawi River, the fort is about four km from the centre. Although it is said to date back to Jammu's legendary founder, Jamboo Loochan, the present structure was built by the Dogras. An old, and highly esteemed, temple to the Goddess Kali can be seen inside the fort. Crowds of worshippers go there on Tuesdays and Sundays.

Amar Mahal Palace

Built in the last century for Raja Amar Singh, the palace is a curious example of French architecture. It's situated just off the Srinagar road on the northern outskirts of town. The palace museum has a family portrait gallery, a library and an important collection of paintings of the Pahari school. It's worth a visit if you have the time. The museum is open from 5 to 7 pm daily and from 8 am to noon on Sundays.

Canals

The Rambir Canal is about two km from the city, it's a favourite stroll in Jammu. The canal leaves the Chenab at Akhnoor, 32 km from Jammu. It provides electricity and irrigation.

ACCOMMODATION

Jammu is very much a transit stop — each night there is a rush for accommodation as people arrive in the city en route to Srinagar or returning from that city. Next morning the buses and trains depart and the city empties out again. The large *Tourist Reception Centre* (tel 5421) on Vir Marg in the city centre has 128 rooms, despite which it is often completely full during the tourist season. Rooms vary in price from Rs 30 a double (D block, Indian toilets) to Rs 45 in the new block. There is also air-con accommodation at Rs 60 a double. Except in H block (Rs 35 a double) and the de-luxe block, you are only allowed to stay for two nights. The dormitory here is just an empty room and even the Rs 2 per night they ask for it is too much — 'about the worst of its kind in India,' according to one traveller.

There is a second *Tourist Reception Centre* at the railway station (tel 8803) and here double rooms cost Rs 25 and the dormitory is Rs 2.75. The railway station also has *Retiring Rooms* at Rs 30 a double or Rs 50 with air-con. Dorm beds here are Rs 6. Note that the railway station is a long way from the town centre — across the Tawi River and several km down the road. The bus station, which is close to the centre, also has *Retiring Rooms* with doubles at Rs 20 and dormitory beds at Rs 2.75.

Jammu's selection of hotels hardly entices one to extend one's stay. The *Hotel Jammu Ashok* (tel 5104, 2084) is one of the government's ITDC chain. Situated close to the Amar Mahal Palace it is on the outskirts of town on the Srinagar side. Singles/doubles are Rs 80/120 with air-con; Rs 60/90 without. The *Hotel Asia* (tel 6373-74-75) is in Nehru Market, only two km from the railway station or airport but some distance from the town centre on the Pathankot side. Singles/doubles are Rs 80/120 with air-con; Rs 50/75 without. Third of Jammu's 'better' hotels is the *Cosmopolitan* (tel 5520) on Vir Marg, directly opposite the tourist centre. Singles/doubles are around Rs 75-100/120-140 with air-con or Rs 40-75/75-100 without. It has absolutely nothing to recommend it apart from its central location — 'an overpriced dump with dirty, non-flushing toilets and non-functioning showers'.

There are many cheaper hotels either along Vir Marg (close to the Tourist Reception Centre) or close to the bus station. The *Picnic*, down the street beside the tourist centre, has doubles from Rs 35 with fan, Rs 40 air-cooled up to Rs 70 with air-con. OK but nothing special. The *Palace Hotel* (tel 6209) on Vir Marg has spartan doubles at Rs 18 while the *Premier* (also on Vir Marg) is similarly basic and slightly cheaper at Rs 15 a double. The *Natraj Hotel* (tel 4150) is beside the Cosmopolitan on Vir Marg and has rooms from Rs 40 to 70 — again nothing very special.

Down beside the bus station, the address is 'below Gumat' since the street is overshadowed by the hill, you'll find the *Astoria Hotel* (tel 2303) and the *Broadway Hotel* (tel 2636) with doubles at around Rs 50. Across the road are the *Diamond* and the *Mahindra*.

PLACES TO EAT

The *Tourist Reception Centre* has a restaurant serving the usual government tourist centre menu. Reasonable sort of food, certainly rather better than its equivalent in Srinagar. Across the road the *Cosmopolitan's* restaurant is air-conditioned and much better than the accompanying hotel — should you want a pleasant meal in cool surroundings and a cold beer to go with it. The *Premier*, just a few doors down, has Chinese and Kashmiri food. There is a collection of little kebab stalls between the two. The railway station and the bus station have the usual station restaurant facilities.

INFORMATION

There is a Government of India Tourist Office (tel 5121) at Gulab Bhawan as well as the Jammu and Kashmir Tourist Office (tel 5324) at the Tourist Reception Centre. The latter is every bit as useless as the main office in Srinagar. To ensure that the minimum possible number of visitors are able to use their facilities they close at 5 pm (before any of the buses from Srinagar arrive in) and open at 9 am (after the buses have all left). The tourist office has a branch at the Jammu-Tawi Railway Station (tel 8803) as well as the main city centre. The GPO is on Pacca Danga. Jammu's population is 160,000.

GETTING AROUND

Jammu has metered taxis, auto-rickshaws and a tempo service between a number of points. From the railway station to the bus station a tempo costs Rs 1.25. The same trip by auto-rickshaw would be Rs 4 to 5. It's only a short distance from the Tourist Reception Centre in the town centre to the bus station, say Rs 2 by auto-rickshaw.

GETTING OUT OF JAMMU

The Indian Airlines office is at the Tourist Reception Centre (tel 2735 or 7088). The airport is seven km out of town. Srinagar buses depart from various locations: A class, de-luxe and air-con buses go from the Tourist Reception Centre. B class buses go from the bus station. Buses also run from the railway station where they meet in-coming trains — thus you can take an overnight train from Delhi and catch a bus to Srinagar as soon as you arrive. Normally the buses depart for Srinagar between 6.30 and 7 am. It is most important that you book your bus on to Srinagar as soon as you arrive in Jammu. Bus fares between Jammu and Srinagar cost Rs 20 (B class), Rs 30 (A class), Rs 55 (super de-luxe) and Rs 90 (air-con).

There are frequent buses from Jammu to Amritsar (Rs 10.50), Pathankot (Rs 4.50, three hours) and other cities to the south. Pathankot is the jumping off point for Dharamsala, Dalhousie and the other Himachal Pradesh hill stations. Buses also operate to Akhnoor, Banihal, Bhadrooh, Katra, Kishtwar, Poonch, Reasi, Ramnagar, Udhampur, Kud and Batote.

AROUND JAMMU

For those with more time, or their own vehicle, there are many places around Jammu or along the road to Srinagar. Prior to the completion of the Jawarhar Tunnel the trip from Jammu to Srinagar took two days with an overnight stop at Batote. Today you make the trip in one day but it's a long haul (10 to 12 hours) with only a couple of rest stops and one lunch stop along the way. Most unusual for an Indian bus trip! There's certainly no time for looking around if you're on the direct bus.

Jammu-Srinagar Road

The route between Jammu and Srinagar is 293 km (183 miles) long. From Jammu the road winds gently up and down to Udhampur (61 km) then climbs steeply to Patnitop (107 km). From here it drops just as steeply to Ramban (158 km), the road follows a picturesque but hazardous river route along this stretch. At Ramban it ascends again to Banihal (187 km) and on to the Jawarhar Tunnel (204 km). The road descends rapidly into the Kashmir Valley, after the tunnel, and runs flat the remaining distance to Srinagar. Places of interest along the road but within Kashmir are covered in the Kashmir section.

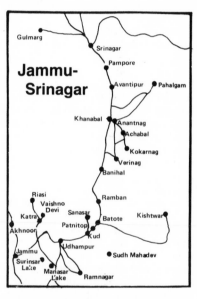

Akhnoor (32 km north-west)

A few km from Jhiri, this is a popular picnic spot where the Chenab River reaches the plains. The Rambir Canal branches off from the Chenab at this point. There is an old fort beside the Chenab. Akhnoor is reached by a regular bus service. This used to be the route to Srinagar from Jammu during the Moghul era. The road passes through Nawshera, Rajauri and Poonch, 246 km from Jammu. Jehangir, who died en route to Kashmir, was buried at Chingas, 36 km before Rajauri. There is a huge Moghul serai at Thana Mandi, near Poonch. The waterfall at Noori Chham, a popular resting place for the Moghul queen Noor Jahan, is 16 km from here.

Basohli (125 km south-east, 53 km from Pathankot)

Situated fairly close to Dalhousie in Himachal Pradesh, Basohli is the birthplace of the Pahari miniature paintings which are so famous in this region.

There are some palace ruins in Basohli and it is a good base for treks. Direct buses run here from Jammu.

Billawar & Sukrala
Billawar is on the road from Udhampur to Dhar, which is near Basohli. The majestic old temple in Billawar is now mostly ruined. There are many interesting ruins of old wells, known as 'baulis' in this area. The temple of Sukrala Devi, with its fine old stone sculpture of the eight-armed Goddess Devi, is picturesquely situated on a hilltop, 10 km from Billawar.

Babor (72 km east)
This site is noted for its five ruined temples with carved figures of the Hindu gods.

Parmandal (39 km south-east, off the Pathankot road)
Another popular picnic spot reached by a regular bus service, Parmandal is the site of an uncompleted rock temple planned, by Maharajah Rambir Singh, as part of a series of pilgrimage centres. The stream that flows from the base of the rock on which the temple is built is held to be particularly sacred. The stone serpent in the central shrine cistern is said to be a unique manifestation of Lord Shiva.

Surinsar Lake (45 km east)
A picturesque lake surrounded by pine trees with a central island.

Mansar Lake (80 km east)
Further, on the same road, beyond Surinsar this lake is also reached by a regular bus service and accommodation is available there in the Dak Bungalow. The legendary hero of the Mahabharata, Anjuna, is said to have shot an arrow into the ground at Mansar. The arrow emerged at Surinsar and thus both lakes were created.

Beside the lake there is a small ruined palace with frescoes on the walls. In May of each year there is a major folk festival at Mansar and later the Chhing festival features wrestling bouts. The mysterious ruins of Mahor Garh, nobody knows who built them or why, are reached from Mansar.

Vaishno Devi (60 km north-west)
This important cave is dedicated to the three mother goddesses of Hinduism. Thousands of pilgrims visit the cave, particularly during the four month pilgrimage season. The cave is 30 metres long and reached by a very narrow entrance. The road terminates at Katra, 48 km from Jammu, and visitors have to make the final, steep, 12 km on foot. There is also a new road which leaves you two km closer to the cave and with considerably less climb to be made. Pilgrims walking to the cave greet each other with the cry 'Jai Mataki' — 'Victory to the Mother Goddess'.

Katra is at the foot of the Trikuta mountains and eight km from Katra is the village of Aghar Jito, site of the annual Kartik Purnima or Jhiri festival. This is held in memory of the hero Bawa Jito whose historic struggle against tyranny is admired today as a symbol of truth and personal courage.

There is a Tourist Bungalow at Katra and a Rest House at Adkunwari, half-way between Katra and the cave. The cave is at 1600 metres. There are regular and de-luxe buses from Jammu to Katra.

Riasi (80 km north-west, beyond Katra)

Three km from the town is the ruined fort of General Zorawar Singh, a controversial warrior best remembered in India for his clashes with the Chinese over Ladakh.

There is a gurdwara, 15 km from Riasi, with some of the oldest known frescoes in the Pahari style. The 400 metre long Shiv Khori cave, another pilgrimage site, is 19 km from Riasi, the last five km must be completed on foot.

Ramnagar (102 km north-east, leaving the Srinagar road at Udhampur)

The Rangmahal, 'palace of colours', has a great number of very colourful and beautiful wall paintings in the Pahari style. The paintings of scenes from Krishna's life are particularly noteworthy. Buses go to Ramnagar from Jammu or Udhampur. The medieval style Hindu temples at Krimchi are 10 km from Udhampur. The temples are notable for their fine carvings and sculpture.

Kud (99 km north-east, on the Srinagar road)

Situated at an altitude of 1738 metres this is a popular lunch stop on the Jammu-Srinagar highway. It's also popular in its own right as a hill resort and has a well known mountain spring, Swami Ki Bauli, 1.5 km from the road. Kud has a Tourist Bungalow and during the summer there is a festival with nightly dancing.

Batote (118 km north-east, on the Srinagar road)

Only 12 km further on and connected to Patnitop and Kud by a number of footpaths, the hill resort of Batote is at an altitude of 1560 metres. This was the overnight stop between Jammu and Srinagar before the opening of the Jawahar tunnel. There is a Tourist Bungalow, tourist huts and several private hotels in Batote. As in Kud there is a famous spring close to the village — the Amrit Chasma is only 2.5 km away.

Patnitop (107 km north-east, on the Srinagar road)

Picturesquely situated at 2024 metres there are many pleasant walks around this popular hill station. It is intended that Patnitop will be the nucleus of tourist developments in this area. There are tourist huts, a Rest House and a Youth Hostel in Patnitop.

Sudh Mahadev (120 km north-east, off the Srinagar road at Kud)
The Shiva temple here attracts many pilgrims during the festival which takes place in July-August each year. The Asad Purnima festival features three days of music, singing and dancing. The holy shrine has a black carved figure of Shiva and Parvati and there is also an interesting inscribed iron trident.

Man Talai, five km from Sudh Mahadev, is of archaeological interest due to the red earthenware and terra-cotta figures discovered here. Gauri Kund, also five km distant, is a small cave associated with Parvati. Sculptures from Hindu mythology can be seen at the Pap Nashni Bauli springs. Shiv Garh is the highest mountain in the area.

Sudh Mahadev is only eight km, by a picturesque walking or jeep track, from Patnitop and Kud. It stands on the banks of the holy Dewak River, held by some to be as sacred as the Ganges. There is a small pilgrim's rest house at Sudh Mahadev which is at an altitude of 1225 metres.

Sanasar (129 km north-east, off the Srinagar road at Patnitop)
At an altitude of 2079 metres the valley of Sanasar has a beautiful meadow where Gujjar shepherds bring their sheep during the warm summer months. Accommodation is available in the Tourist Bungalow, in tourist huts and in several private hotels.

Bhadarwah (204 km north-east, off the Srinagar road at Batote)
Every two years a procession of pilgrims starts from this beautful, high altitude valley and walks to the 4400 metre high Kaplash Lake. The pilgrimage takes place two weeks after the Rakhi Purnima festival and is followed a week later by Mela Patt, a three-day festival in Bhadarwah. There are bus services from Jammu to Bhadarwah, the road leaves the Srinagar highway at Batote and heads east towards Kishtwar. A road then branches south-east to Bhadarwah. There is a rest house in this scenic location.

Kishtwar (216 km north-east, off the Srinagar road at Batote)
Well off the Jammu-Srinagar road, Kishtwar is connected to Srinagar by a trekking route which goes through Banderkot, Dhadpeth, Mughal Maidan, Chatur, Sinthan and Daksum, crossing the 3797 metre Sinthan Pass. You can also trek from Kishtwar into Zanskar, as detailed in the Zanskar section.

Kisthwar is sited on a plateau above the Chenab River and below the Nagin Sheer glacier. It is noted for the fine saffron grown in the area and for the many waterfalls close by. A fall only three km from the town drops over 700 metres in a series of seven cascades.

The pilgrimage site of Sarthal Devi, with its 18-armed goddess statue, is 19 km from the town. Kishtwar also has the tombs of two important Moslem saints. Just over 100 km beyond Kisthwar are the blue sapphire mines of Paddar, situated at an altitude of over 4000 metres.

Jawarhar Tunnel (200 km from Jammu, 93 km from Srinagar)
Until the completion of the tunnel, Srinagar and Kashmir were often totally cut off from the rest of India during the winter months. The tunnel has two separate passages, each over 2500 metres long. It's at an altitude of 2500 metres and the condition of the road is terrible! Windscreen wipers are needed in the tunnel since it 'rains' inside. The tunnel not only ensured that Kashmir was accessible year round but also took half a day off the trip between Jammu and Srinagar. From Banihal, 17 km before the tunnel, you are already entering the Kashmiri region — many people speak Kashmiri as well as Dogri and many of the houses are of the traditional Kashmiri style. As soon as you pass through the tunnel you are in the Vale of Kashmir and its green lushness is strikingly different from the other side of the range.

Kashmir

Kashmir is one of India's most beautiful and touristically popular regions and has been since the time of the great Moghul emperors. It's probably most famous for the houseboats on picturesque Dal Lake, you've not really been to Kashmir until you've stayed on one. There's a lot more to the Kashmir Valley than just lazing on board, however. Around the capital, Srinagar, there are a number of interesting mosques, temples and forts and, of course, the delightful Moghul gardens — laid out in formal patterns hundreds of years ago and every bit as beautiful today. But you have to get away from Srinagar, up to the hill stations around the valley, to really enjoy Kashmir. Pahalgam, Gulmarg and Sonamarg are all interesting in themselves but they also serve as the jumping off points for Kashmir's many trekking possibilities.

HISTORY
Due to its isolation, in a high valley of the Himalayas, Kashmir has developed an independent cultural and historical tradition over the centuries. Until the arrival of Islam in the 14th century and the 1586 conquest of the region by the Moghul Emperor Akbar, Kashmir was ruled by local dynasties. Earlier still Buddhism had become established in Kashmir with, as in so many other places in India, Ashoka as its main promulgator. Around the time of the birth of Christ, the third Buddhist Congress took place in Kashmir and missionaries were sent out to neighbouring regions of Central Asia, Tibet and China.

In the following centuries Buddhism lost its influence and by the 7th century had almost been replaced by Hinduism. Hind dynasties followed in rapid succession through the middle ages but they always exercised tolerance for Buddhism. The Kashmiris were gradually changing to the Islamic religion and a series of Moslem rulers commenced from the 1300s. One of the best known and most respected of these local rulers was Zain-ul-Abidin, whose tomb can still be seen by the Jhelum River in Srinagar and who was generally known as Badshah, 'the great king'. He ruled from 1421 to 1472 and was a considerable contrast to his father, Sultan Sikander, who, with the guidance of a fanatical prime minister, persecuted countless Hindus and virtually ended the historical religious tolerance of the valley.

With the conquest of the valley by the Moghuls, Kashmir entered into a period of stable political conditions and great cultural activity. The Moghuls chose Kashmir as their summer residence and built many fine gardens, particularly under Jehangir who took the art of designing Moghul gardens to its greatest heights.

As the Moghul period entered its time of decline the government of Kashmir became practically independent and in 1756 Kashmir fell to Afghanistan and then in 1819 was taken over by the Sikhs, who called upon the Kashmiris to aid them in the struggle against the brutal Afghan rule. The

Sikh General Gulab Singh was given Kashmir by the British as reward for his neutrality in the war between the British and the Sikhs.

Gilgit, Hunza, Nagar and Chitral were added to this region and, under the rule of the Hindu Dogra dynasty, the state of Jammu and Kashmir arrived at more-or-less its present shape. In 1947, with independence from Britain and the partition of India and Pakistan, Kashmir assumed the role as thorn-in-the-side of India-Pakistan relations which it has held ever since. Since Kashmir was a 'Princely State' and, theoretically, already independent the British could not simply grant it independence like most of India but had to persuade it to join one side or the other. Kashmir became one of the three states, the others were Hyderabad and the tiny principality of Junagadh, whose rulers could not or would not opt for India or Pakistan but clutched at the feeble hope of remaining independent.

Hari Singh's decision not to join either country, or rather, some would say, indecision since he was far from being a strong or decisive ruler, was a fateful one. Kashmir was predominantly Moslem so on the basis of religion it should clearly have gone to Pakistan. Furthermore it was geographically more closely aligned to Pakistan than to India. When the Pakistanis realised that Hari Singh, who was a Hindu, may not have joined India but certainly did not intend to join Pakistan they organised an unofficial takeover bid. Pathan tribesmen from the North-West Frontier region moved into Kashmir and internal revolts soon had Hari Singh's army in tatters. He turned to India for assistance but the price was an obvious one — Hari Singh took Kashmir into the Indian union. It might have been too late for Indian troops to save Kashmir but the tribesmen had been so busy looting along the way that they had still not arrived in Srinagar when the first Indian troops were flown in. Nevertheless a full scale war between India and Pakistan was soon underway and was not halted until a UN cease-fire came into effect on 1 January 1949. A substantial part of Kashmir was in Pakistani hands but the Vale of Kashmir was firmly under Indian control.

At first Kashmir was run as an autonomous region with its own government and president. Karan Singh, son of the Maharajah, was the first to hold this office, but in 1957 Kashmir was formally made part of the Indian union, despite Pakistani protests. Pakistan has repeatedly requested that a referendum be held in Kashmir but although at one time India agreed they would eventually hold such a referendum there has always been some reason why it could not be conducted. In 1965 India and Pakistan were again at war and again the Pakistanis nearly captured Srinagar but although the cease-fire line was pushed back in several places the status quo remained essentially unchanged. In 1971, during the Bangladesh conflict, it was India that took the offensive and Pakistan that was pushed back.

In 1962 the Indians found themselves involved with a different foe, the Chinese. So neglected was the Ladakh region of the state that the Chinese actually managed to construct a high altitude road right across the area they now hold without India being aware of it. When the conflict had eventually ground to a halt another cease-fire line was drawn across the region. Today Kashmir, which includes Ladakh, is divided between three countries and essentially related people are artifically divided by enforced nationalities. There are no roads open across the borders of Kashmir and no official trade takes place beween the Indian and other parts of Kashmir. Given freedom of choice the Kashmiris would probably opt for independence as a sort of 'buffer state' between India and Pakistan, with their borders open to both countries. Barring that choice they would probably prefer Pakistan to India but, given the impossibility of that dream today they appear to make the most of life in India.

INFORMATION
Srinagar stands at an altitude of 1768 metres and has a population of about 450,000. There are a number of banks in Srinagar and money changing facilities are also available at the airport and in several of the larger hotels. The GPO, with poste restante facilities, is on the Bund, quite near the Tourist Reception Centre. The telegraph office and the telephone office are on Maulana Azad Rd (Hotel Rd). Indian Airline's office is in the TRC (tel 3538, 3270 & 6242) and is open from 10 am to 5 pm. The J&K Road Transport Corporation is also located at the TRC.

Tourist Office
The Srinagar office of the J&K Department of Tourism is at the Tourist Reception Centre — a large complex which houses the various tourist departments, Indian Airlines, a restaurant/cafeteria, an accommodation block, hotel and houseboat booking counters and the J&K Road Transport Corporation booking offices. It's also the departure point for J&K RTC tour buses and the buses to Jammu and Leh.

Despite the importance of tourism in Kashmir and the imposing size of the tourist office it's one of the worst in India. They're virtually devoid of printed information, the various people working there are generally ill-informed, unknowledgeable and often unhelpful and unfriendly into the bargain! They also insist (heavily) that all new arrivals in Srinagar should book houseboats and hotels through the tourist office. This is, of course, completely unnecessary and in any case you'll only be steered towards the hotels and houseboats of 'friends' of the desk staff. Plus you'll probably end up paying more for houseboats than you would if you negotiated it yourself. It's a very poor tourist office.

Tony Wheeler

SEASONS
Kashmir, with its lush vegetation and wide variety of fruits, presents a different face for every season. The almond trees blossom in March but it's the

chinars, which leaf in April, that really herald spring. Strawberries and cherries are on sale in May, followed by apricots in June and apples in July. The early autumn brings pears, pomegranates and walnuts. Waterbirds, heading south for the winter, pause in Kashmir in great numbers. Finally the leaves fall and by November or December the first snow can be expected around the valley.

PEOPLE
Kashmir has a population of about four million of whom about half a million live in Srinagar. The population is predominantly Moslem and more related to central Asia than to India in both appearance and temperament. They have a terrible reputation for trickiness although in actual fact they're probably no worse (or better) than any other group of people in India (or Asia)! Nevertheless Indians have many little proverbs about the Kashmiris, like 'Kashmiris are so fond of the truth they'll rarely part with it.' In turn the Kashmiris think of India as quite a separate country — you 'return to India' when you head south to Jammu. Despite its Moslem majority Kashmir has a strong Hindu minority well known for their intellectual pursuits. Nehru, India's first prime minister, was a Kashmiri 'pandit' and many of the closest advisers of both Nehru and his daughter, Indira Gandhi, were Kashmiris.

KASHMIRI FOOD
Kashmiri cuisine has some special variations from normal Indian food although it is basically of the north Indian type. Some Kashmiri dishes you may come across include:
Gushtaba — pounded and spiced meat balls cooked in a yoghurt sauce. *Rista* are very similar to gushtaba but without the flavoured sauce.
Roghan josh — also fairly common elsewhere in north India this is, in its most basic form, just curried mutton but a good roghan josh will be cooked in yoghurt (curd) with a careful blend of exotic spices and added ingredients. *Yaknee* is similar to roghan josh.
Tabak maz is fried meat, not spiced at all. *Marchwangan kurma* is a hot mutton curry. *Methi kurma* is vegetables with chopped intestines — it tastes much better than it sounds. *Karam sag* is made from the popular Dal Lake vegetable known as lak — it's a bit like giant spinach. *Nadru yekni* is made from lotuses, cooked with curd. *Kashmiri nan* is the usual flat Indian bread but with sultanas and nuts baked into it. Kashmiri nan is really delicious but Kashmiri bread is very good to start with. The Kashmiris also make a fruit and nut pillau — a bit like fried fruit salad! Popular vegetables in Kashmir include *bartha* — minced aubergines — and *brindi* — lady fingers.

Drinks Kashmir tea is a fragrant, delicate blend flavoured with cardoman and ginger — a delightfully thirst quenching drink. Quite possibly the best tea in India? A really good cup of this *kahwa* tea will be brewed in a samovar and have grated almonds in it. It's usually drunk without milk. Soft drinks, freighted up from the plains, tend to be expensive but there's a delicious local brand of apple juice known as Apco. It's a great change from the sickly Indian soft drinks and costs Rs 2 to 2.50, the same as regular soft drinks in Kashmir. Take care with Kashmiri water, especially if you suspect it may have come straight from Dal Lake!

KASHMIRI HANDICRAFTS

Kashmir is famous for its wide variety of often very beautiful handicrafts. You'll have a hard heart and tight wallet if something doesn't convince you to take it home! Some of the better known items include:

Carpets One of the best known, and most expensive, Kashmiri handicrafts is carpet weaving. The art of weaving carpets first came from Samarkand in central Asia and was later modified by artisans from Iran. Zain-ul-Abidin is credited with first introducing the skill to Kashmir. Carpets come in a variety of sizes — three by five foot, four by six foot and so on. They are either made of pure wool, wool with a small percentage of silk to give a sheen (known as 'silk touch') or pure silk. The latter are more decorative than intended for hard wear. To see just how decorative Kashmiri carpets can be as a wall hanging pay a visit to the restaurant in the Broadway Hotel. Kashmiri carpets are not cheap — expect to pay from Rs 5000 for a good quality four by six carpet and don't be surprised if the price is more than twice that level. Beware of cheap imitations from Amritsar and of false knotting.

Kashmir also has some cheaper, more country crafted rugs such as the embroidered numdas and the applique like gabbas. You can compare the different types in the handicrafts emporiums.

Papier Mache As instantly recognisable as a product of Kashmir are the papier mache items. The basic papier mache article, made in a mould, is then painted and polished in successive layers until the final intricate design is produced. Prices are generally dependant upon the complexity and quality of the painted design and on the amount of gold leaf used. The gold leaf is applied in tiny pieces to produce the leaf design or other pattern. Papier mache is made into bowls, cups, containers, jewel boxes, letter holders, tables, lamps, coasters, trays and so on. Prices can be as low as Rs 10 for a cheap bowl to several hundred for some large, fine quality piece. Production is very much a cottage industry with the moulded 'rough' form being made in one place, the painting being done in another. It's very easy to arrange to go to a papier mache 'factory' to see how it's done.

Leather & Fur You can have shoes or boots or leather coats made to measure in just a few days in Srinagar. The beautifully embroidered suede coats are particularly interesting but you have to put your conscience in the back seat when it comes to the fur trim. The same goes for the many fur coats — fur should be left on the backs of its original owners. You can, however, find sheepskin lined or trimmed coats. Although Kashmiri leather, suede or sheepskin may look very fine the quality is often abysmally low — look carefully before buying. Expect to pay Rs 400 to Rs 1000 for a coat, good boots can be made for Rs 200 to Rs 400.

Wood Carvings Intricately carved designs are a hallmark of Kashmiri wood-craft. You can see the complex relief work on every houseboat. Look for tables, chests, boxes and screens. Inlaid ivory is often incorporated into the design.

Shawls & Embroidery Kashmiri shawls are noted for the extreme fineness of the cream coloured goats' wool known as pashmina and for the intricate embroidery work. Shawl making has been a Kashmiri speciality for over 500 years. Expect to pay from Rs 100 to Rs 200 for a shawl. Embroidery of all types is a Kashmiri craft — embroidered suede coats or bags, embroidered shirts or dress material, they're all popular items.

Honey The cardinal rule when buying honey in Kashmir is taste it first. Kashmiri substitutes for the real thing include sugar dissolved in water or alcohol! Do not, however, be put off by the packaging — Kashmiri honey can be very good although the best honey will be found at small stalls reached only by shikara. You may also find lotus blossom honey as well as the normal variety.

Other Srinagar's hordes of tailors ('I am just like Savile Row, only cheaper') search you out on your houseboats if you don't go to them. They'll make anything from a shirt to a suit. Dried fruit may be a Kashmiri speciality but it's a very expensive one. Much jewellery is really from Rajasthan. There's also a thriving business in Tibetan jewellery and other artifacts. Nice coarsely hand knitted sweaters in grey or dark brown wool are available from Rs 75, from Rs 100 for cardigans. Saffron, the highly fragrant orange coloured spice and dye is a Kashmiri speciality. Pure saffron is very expensive and it's an easy product to adulterate so take care.

Places to Shop
There are a whole string of Government Handicraft Emporiums scattered around Srinagar but the main one is housed in the fine old British Residency buildings by the Bund. Here you'll find a representative selection of reasonably good quality items at reasonable prices. Even if you don't buy there, and take advantage of the government's quality guarantee, it's a good idea to familiarise yourself with what's available here.

Other good shopping areas include along the Boulevard by Dal Lake where some of the flashiest shops can be found. The Bund also has an interesting selection of shops including *Suffering Moses* where you'll find some particularly high quality items. The Government Central Market, across Badshah Bridge, has a variety of stalls and again some government quality and price control is exercised. Hari Singh St, near the Amira Kadal Bridge, is a popular older shopping area, as are Polo View Rd and Lambert Lane in the centre. There are literally hundreds of other shops scattered all over Srinigar and if you don't fall prey to those persuasive salesmen they'll pursue you all the way back to your houseboat — countless shikaras patrol Dal Lake like shoals of sharks, loaded down with the same items you'll find in the shops.

Kashmir Dress
The traditional way of coping with the bitter cold of a Kashmiri winter is with a 'kangri'. A kangri is an earthenware bowl which, fitted in a wicker container, is carried in front of you under a 'pheran', the enveloping Kashmiri cape. A small fire is built in the kangri and you have personal, portable central-heating! Beware of burning embers falling out of the bowl; long term kangri carriers usually have the burns to prove it. Equally a vital part of a Kashmiri's existence is the hookah (hubble-bubble) pipe — they're in every shop, in every shikara.

ACCOMMODATION
Srinagar has a great number of hotels apart from its well known floating hostelries. If you want something at the very bottom of the price scale or, conversely, at the top end of the luxury scale, you may find it easier on dry land.

Accommodation in Srinagar — bottom end
There are cheap hotels scattered all around Srinagar although those around the Lal Chowk area can be very noisy. The best bargains in cheap hotels are probably to be found actually on Dal Lake, scattered amongst the houseboats. Not only are the prices pleasantly low but they're also much quieter than streetside hotels. Prices in these cheapies can be very variable depending on season and demand but can go as low as Rs 5 or 10 per person.

Check the *Latif Guest House* or the *Hotel Sundowna* — the latter has rooms as low as Rs 15, fairly spartan but quite OK and good food. Right next door there's the *Hotel Savoy* with rooms from Rs 25 (spartan) through Rs 40 to Rs 50. Again the food is good. A little up market from these places — and further up the channel towards Dal Gate — is *Hotel Heaven Canal* with doubles from Rs 50 to 80.

If you want your feet on solid ground, but cheaply, try the friendly *Tibetan Guest House* above the Lhasa Restaurant, just off the Boulevard. *Zero Inn*, by Zero Bridge, is also reasonably quiet but rather more expensive at Rs 50 or more for a double. Kashmir is not a cheap place for accommodation by Indian standards.

The J&K tourist office operates four accommodation units in Srinagar.

Right at the Tourist Reception Centre (tel 6107) there are retiring rooms, rooms and suites with prices ranging from Rs 60 to Rs 80. They are intended only as short stay places (rates double after 48 hours) despite which they are generally full up during the season. The two J&K operated hotels are the *Lalla Rukh Hotel* (tel 72373) and the *Budshah Hotel* (tel 76053) both in Lal Chow, a noisy part of town. Finally there are the tourist huts near the Chasma Shahi gardens. These come complete with kitchens and cooking equipment but are only really usable if you have your own transport. They cost around Rs 200 a night for a double and are booked through the Tourist Reception Centre.

The Srinagar *Youth Hostel* is across the river from the town centre, near the museum. Nightly charges are just Rs 2 and reservations must be made through the Education Department. There is a campsite just beyond the Nagin Lake causeway, only a short distance before the Hazratbal Mosque. A good place if you've come to Kashmir with your own vehicle.

Accommodation in Srinagar — top end
Srinagar's top of the list establishment is the *Oberoi Palace Hotel*, the one-time palace of the Maharajah of Kashmir. It's situated off the Boulevard, several km around the lake from Dal Gate. The actual building is rather uninspired, particularly if you've seen the sumptuous palace hotels of Rajasthan, but the gardens in front of the hotel provide superb views out over the lake. The Oberoi Palace (tel 2231-34 & 5641-42) has 110 rooms with singles from Rs 320, doubles from Rs 520.

Much more central is *Nedou's Hotel* (tel 73015-16) on Hotel Rd, also known as Maulana Azad Rd. It's only a short stroll from the Tourist Reception Centre or the central shopping area. Nedou's is a little decrepit looking and has 79 rooms with singles/doubles from Rs 150/200. Almost next door, and looking as new as Nedou's is old, you'll find the *Broadway* (tel 5611). The 97 rooms in this pleasant, modern hotel cost Rs 170/280 for singles/doubles and it has a popular restaurant.

Srinagar has many other hotels in the upper class bracket — some in the central part of town but most along the Boulevard looking out on Dal Lake. Some of these hotels include the *Hotel Jehangir* (tel 73013-14) just across Budshah Bridge from the centre. Here singles/doubles cost Rs 100/200. Along the Boulevard there's the *Hotel Boulevard* (tel 74964, 76195) with singles/doubles from Rs 120/150 and *Hotel Shahanshah* (tel 75856) at Rs 160/240.

Other hotels along the Boulevard include the pleasant *Hotel Paradise*. The *Nehru Guest House* is opposite Nehru Park while *Hotel Holy Night* is actually on Dal Lake. *Mazda Hotel* is on the Boulevard while *Hotel Green View* is again down by Nehru Park.

Houseboats & How to Find Them
Staying in a houseboat is one of the prime attractions of a visit to Kashmir.

They are lined up in colourful ranks in Dal Lake, across from the Boulevard, or along the Jhelum River. Those who want a little more isolation and peace can also find them at Nagin Lake.

Houseboats originated in the Victorian era as a superbly British solution to a tricky political problem. The British liked Kashmir but the Maharajah wouldn't allow them to buy land to build houses on. So they had houseboats built and the style has hardly changed from the first boat in 1888 right down to boats being built today. They're a great escape from the noise and hassle which any Indian city, and Srinagar is no exception, seem to have an over ample supply of. As soon as you get out on the lake the traffic and confusion simply fades away — they're very relaxing.

Houseboats are also highly entertaining — you just sit out on the verandah on the front of your boat and life passes by in front of you. A flock of ducks, children barely old enough to walk (but quite adept at paddling), hookah smoking shikara men, fat ladies in saris, travellers and freaks (often paddling themselves in circles), they all pass by you. You don't have to go to the shops — the shops come to you. Jewellers, papier mache dealers, incredibly persuasive tailors, even the local supermarket will turn up — 'you want beer, soap, cold drinks, toilet paper?' And if none of those appeal — 'hashish?' Remember that it has been said that houseboat owners make their profit not from the room charges but from the kickbacks on what their visitors buy!

Officially houseboats come in five categories with official prices for each category. These are, for accommodation plus all meals:

De-luxe or 5-star	single/double	Rs 170/250 per day
A class		Rs 115/170
B class		Rs 80/130
C class		Rs 50/90
D class or 'doonga boats'		Rs 35/45
D class 'lodging only' for whole boat		Rs 30

First of all what is a houseboat and what do you get for your money? Basically it's a flat bottomed, very stationary boat something between 20 and 40 metres long and three to six metres wide. They follow a very standard pattern in their design — you board the boat by a small verandah and then enter the living room/lounge area. It's inevitably furnished in a style you could describe as 'English chintz'. From the lounge you enter the dining room followed by the small kitchen area — although food is generally prepared in a nearby kitchen boat. Stairs lead up from here to the rooftop sundeck. Finally a corridor leads back along one side of the boat to two or three bedrooms, each with its own bathroom and toilet.

The 'all-inclusive' price will include your room, all meals (breakfast, lunch and dinner), tea at least a couple of times a day, and transport back and forth between your boat and the shore in the houseboat's shikara. Of course getting back is only possible if your shikara man happens to be waiting at the landing. Generally you'll have to take, and pay for, one of the shikaras waiting there. Houseboats are usually owned in groups of two, three or more with one shikara to serve them all and also one kitchen boat (or land-based equivalent) to feed them all.

The top 5-star boats will be very luxurious indeed with new furniture and fittings, chandeliers in the dining room, radio or even TV, running hot water and so on. Moving down the scale the drop in standards is usually a matter of age rather than facilities — houseboats all look remarkably alike, just younger or older. Doonga boats are, however, usually much smaller, often just one-roomed and with primitive sanitation facilities.

The tourist office 'official' prices are actually nowhere near as rigid as their neat categorisation might indicate. For a start the boats vary within their categories — there's 5-star and **5-STAR**! Similarly some run down A class boats are no better than some well kept C class boats. Secondly there's competition — even at the height of the season there are a lot more houseboat berths than visitors and out of season the competition is intense to try and lure you aboard! End result is prices are generally subject to negotiation. At the worst you should be able to get away with paying the level that applies in the category one step down.

When enquiring about houseboats remember that this is Kashmir. It's necessary to pin them down on every little detail or be prepared for arguments when it comes to departure time. Find out what you can expect for the meals (how many eggs for breakfast?), if you opt not to have dinners some nights check what the reduction will be. Most people decide to have lunch off the boat every day. Make certain the shikara trips to shore are included — if not remember that's it's only 50p to get across from boat to shore, so don't pay too much for a few ferry rides. If you're in a lower class boat without hot water check that they'll supply buckets of water in the morning — Srinagar is a little chilly for washing in cold water. Check if your boat is hooked up to the mains water supply or not, water pumped straight from the lake is definitely not drinkable.

It's virtually impossible to recommend particular boats. Since you're much more 'contained' in a boat than in a hotel little things can make all the difference. If the regular cook goes on holidays and the food standards fall you're stuck with it since you can't walk to the restaurant at the corner! Similarly a friendly shikara man can make all the difference to an otherwise unexceptional boat — he has to bring you washing water, make the tea and bring it across, shuttle you back and forth from boat to shore. Hopefully with a smile. Food even in the best boats can get monotonous and since a C class boat may well be sharing the same kitchen boat as a 5-star boat there is not likely to be a great difference between categories.

Finally how to find a houseboat. Don't do it through the tourist office — you're likely to end up paying the maximum price and your choice of boats is probably restricted to the friends of the man behind the counter. It's much easier just to drift down to one of the landing 'ghats' and either let somebody grab you or take a shikara and go looking for a suitable berth. The kids at the ghats always know which boats have vacancies and by the time you've looked into half a dozen you'll have a pretty good idea what your money buys you. There are hundreds upon hundreds of houseboats so you can always shift to another if you find yours isn't such a bargain after all, or if the food is not to your taste.

Marriage in Kashmir
If you spend long in Kashmir you may get an opportunity to see a large Islamic wedding. The ceremonies often take place over several days and because of the huge cost involved it is not unusual for several sisters to be married on the same day.

The festivities take place not in houses but in lavish tents which are erected in gardens. Men and women are kept strictly separate during the festivities. Before the wedding day the bridegroom is occupied with the monetary gifts of friends and relatives. On the evening before the actual ceremony he goes, with the entire wedding company, to the house of the bride to sign the 'nika' or marriage contract. Only men take part in this ceremony and the bride is represented by her father. The contract is sealed in the presence of a mullah and a small sugarball or 'shirien' is distributed to each guest. Late into the night a feast is held to celebrate the union.

The next morning the bride in a draped litter or in a car with draped windows and the bridegroom on a horse are accompanied by the whole wedding party to the bridegroom's house. The bridegroom generally gives his future wife a very valuable item of jewellery as a wedding present, often a massive golden necklace and armband.

PLACES TO EAT
Srinagar is not a terribly exciting place for eating out — perhaps it's because so many people take their meals on their houseboats, so that restaurants have not had a chance to develop. Surprisingly also nobody has yet come up with the logical follow up to the houseboats — a floating restaurant.

The *Oberoi Palace Hotel* does a very superior buffet dinner at Rs 50 and at lunch time you can dine (or just have a snack) on their sweeping lawn. A la carte most dishes are in the Rs 15 to Rs 25 bracket. The *Broadway* also has a buffet (Rs 40) in their pleasantly carpet-decorated restaurant. Food here (on the non-buffet nights) is quite reasonably priced and you can sample quite possibly the best kahwa tea in Srinagar — an expensive treat.

Ahdoo's, which fronts on to the Bund and backs on to Residency Rd, has been said to have some of the best Kashmiri food in Srinagar but generally fails to live up to its reputation. Most dishes are under Rs 10. Across the road the *Grand* has a similar menu. Others in this area include the *Capri Bar & Restaurant* and the *Premier*.

Just off the Boulevard the Tibetan run *Lhasa Restaurant* does quite good Chinese-Tibetan food. A complete meal for two will cost Rs 40 to Rs 50. Further back towards Dal Gate, on the Boulevard, there's the *Shamyana* with good vegetarian food and reasonable prices.

Right in the central area the *Indian Coffee House* is a good place for a coffee and a chat — the food line here is rather limited: quite good vegetable cutlets and rather so-so masala dosas. Right across the road the *Hollywood Cafe* has much, much better food than its plain appearance would suggest. Seekh kebab or kanti roast make an excellent lunch here and their french fries are superb by any standards. Plus good cakes or snacks at other times of day.

Ice cream is not bad at *Dimples*, either in the centre (opposite the Hollywood) or by Zero Bridge. The latter is known as the *Little Hut* and also has good milkshakes. There's a good selection of Indian sweets at *Shakti Sweets* also by the Hollywood. The cafe at the Tourist Reception Centre is terrible but you can get early morning snacks from the stalls which set up opposite the TRC for the early bus departures.

GETTING TO SRINAGAR
Flights Indian Airlines fly to Srinagar from New Delhi (Rs 377), Chandigarh (Rs 319), Amritsar (Rs 215), Jammu (Rs 104) and there are flights operating from Srinagar to Leh and back. Flights are more frequent during the summer tourist season, at that time there will probably be a Delhi-Chandigarh-Jammu-Srinagar flight and a Jammu-Srinagar flight by HS-748 each day. A 737 will also fly Delhi-Amritsar-Srinagar and there will probably be another direct 737 and an Airbus. Flight time from Delhi on the direct flights is about an hour and ten minutes. As usual in India you should book your flight as early as possible.

At Srinagar airport, which is about 13 km out of the city, there is a fairly chaotic scene as the Tourist Office tries to register every incoming foreigner and insists that you book any accommodation through the Tourist Reception Centre. It's the first place where J&K Tourism do their best to make themselves unpopular. There's an airport bus to the Tourist Reception Centre in Srinagar which costs Rs 4. By taxi it costs Rs 30.

In Srinagar the Indian Airlines office is at the Tourist Reception Centre (tel 73538 & 73270) and is open from 10 am to 5 pm. It's also at the Tourist Reception Centre in Jammu (tel 2735 & 7088).

Train & Bus It's 880 km from Delhi to Srinagar although almost everybody coming up from Delhi, or other Indian cities, by land will come through Jammu (591 km from Delhi) from where the buses run daily to Srinagar. By train there are about four services a day from Delhi or New Delhi to Jammu Tawi, across the river from Jammu. The trip takes nine to 13 hours, usually overnight, and costs about Rs 33 in 2nd class, Rs 120 in 1st class. There are also buses from Delhi but people making the trip by road will most probably be coming via Chandigarh, Amritsar or the Himachal Pradesh hill stations.

Buses leave Jammu early in the morning (between 6.30 and 7 am) for the 10 to 12 hour trip to Srinagar in the Kashmir Valley. Bus fares are Rs 20 (B class), Rs 30 (A class), Rs 55 (super de-luxe) and Rs 90 (air-con). B class buses seat two and three, A class two and two, super de-luxe two and two in individual seats with headrests. Although there are many buses (a veritable armada leaves Jammu each morning) you should book a seat as soon as you arrive in Jammu. The same applies from Srinagar as the day before departure all seats may be sold out. There are also taxis operating between the two cities at Rs 110 per seat or Rs 440 for the whole taxi.

For information about booking trains from Jammu while in Srinagar enquire at the railways office in the Tourist Reception Centre or at N D Radha Kishen & Sons, Railway Out Agency, Badshah Chowk, Srinagar (tel 2146). Bus bookings are made at the Tourist Reception Centre (tel 2698), allow plenty of time as the booking system is archaic.

GETTING AROUND SRINAGAR
There is a wide choice of transport available either on the lake or out and around it, plus a variety of tours. The tour buses are generally much more comfortable than the usual run of over-crowded local buses and, since many of them offer one-way fares, they can be used for getting out to hill stations in the valley. The best known Kashmiri transport is, of course, the shikara:

Shikaras These are the graceful, long boats which crowd the Srinagar lakes. They're used for getting back and forth from the houseboats or for longer tours. Officially there is a standard fare for every trip around the lake and these are prominently posted at the main landings (ghats); in practice the fares can be quite variable. To be shuttled across to your houseboat should cost Rs 2 in a covered ('full spring seats') shikara but the kids who are always out for a little pocket money will happily paddle you across for 50p or less in a basic, open shikara. Of course late at night, particularly if it is raining, the tables are turned and getting back to your houseboat at a reasonable price may require a little ingenuity! If you hire a shikara by the day or for a longer trip, count on about Rs 7 or Rs 8 per hour.

Try paddling a shikara yourself sometime — it's nowhere near as easy as it looks. You'll spend lots of time going round in circles. If your houseboat hasn't got one to spare some children passing by will find you a boat for Rs 4 or Rs 5 per day.

Taxis & Autorickshaws There are stands for these at the Tourist Reception Centre and other strategic locations in town. Srinagar's taxi-wallahs are extremely reluctant to use their meters so you'll have to bargain hard. Count on about Rs 5 for a taxi from the Tourist Reception Centre to Dal Gate (Rs 3 by autorickshaw) or Rs 30 to the airport. For longer trips the official fares are all posted by the stands.

Buses The Jammu & Kashmir Road Transport Corporation buses go from the Tourist Reception Centre while private buses operate from a variety of stands in Srinagar. Certain major long distance routes are reserved for the J&K buses (Jammu, Leh, etc) but others are open for competition and there will be a great number of buses operating.

Tours The J&K Road Transport Corporation operate a number of daily tours from the Tourist Reception Centre. Private bus companies, particularly KMDA (Kashmir Motor Drivers' Association) also have a number of tours. The J&K RTC tours are:

Pahalgam	daily	Rs 20 round trip, Rs 10 one way
Daksum	daily	Rs 20 round trip, Rs 10 one way
Gulmarg	daily	Rs 21 round trip, Rs 12.50 one way
Aharbal	Tues, Thur, Sun	Rs 16
Verinag	Wed, Sun	Rs 16
Wular Lake	Mon, Wed, Fri	Rs 16.50
Yusmarg	Tues, Thur, Sun	Rs 13.50 round trip, Rs 7.50 one way
Sonamarg	daily	Rs 18.50 round trip, Rs 10 one way
Moghul Gardens	twice daily	Rs 11

KMDA tours include Pahalgam (Rs 16 round trip, Rs 12 one way), Aharbal (Rs 12), Verinag (Rs 10), Wular Lake (Rs 9.50), Sonamarg (Rs 13) and Moghul Gardens and Shankaracharya Hill (Rs 6).

Bicycles Seeing Srinagar by bicycle is a surprisingly pleasant way of getting around — economical too. You can hire bikes for Rs 4 per day from bicycle shops. There are several along the Boulevard close to Dal Gate. Pleasant trips to be made include:

Round Dal Lake — an all day trip going by the Moghul gardens. It's particularly pleasant around the north of the lake where the villages are still relatively untouched.

Across the lake — you can ride right across the lake on the causeway, a nice trip since there are no problems with vehicle traffic and there is plenty of opportunity to observe the lake life without being in a boat.

Nagin Lake — you can ride out to the Hazratbal Mosque via Nagin Lake and then make a complete loop around the lake on the way back. This trip can easily be combined with a trip along the Jhelum, taking in the various mosques close to the river. The streets here are very narrow so vehicles keep away and bike riding is pleasant.

SRINAGAR

The capital of Jammu and Kashmir and the largest city in the state, Srinagar is famous for its canals, houseboats and Moghul gardens. All the distances to the places of interest described below are from the Tourist Reception Centre in town. Note that admission to all the Moghul gardens is free, except for the Chasma Shahi which costs 50p. The gardens are all open from sunrise to sunset.

The art of designing formal gardens, which the Moghul emperors expended such time and energy upon, reached its zenith in Kashmir. The Moghul gardens in Agra or Lahore may be very fine but only in Kashmir is the formal beauty of the gardens matched by the natural beauty of the surrounding countryside. The gardens follow a standard pattern with a central channel carrying water through the descending terraces in a delightful series of cascades, falls and pools.

Dal Lake

Dal Lake is, initially, one of the most confusing parts of Srinagar for it's not really one lake at all, but three. Furthermore much of it is hardly what you would expect a lake to be like — it's a maze of intricate waterways and channels, floating islands of vegetation, houseboats that look so firmly moored they could almost be islands and hotels on islands which look like they could simply float away.

Dal Lake lies immediately to the east and north of Srinagar and stretches for over five km. The lake is divided into Gagribal, Lokut Dal and Bod Dal by a series of causeways. Nagin Lake, which is usually thought of as a separate lake, is also divided from Dal Lake only by a causeway. The causeways are suitable for walkers and bicycles only so they make a very pleasant way of seeing the lake without having to worry about traffic or shikaras. The main causeway across the lake carries the water pipeline for Srinagar's mains water supply. Dal Gate, at the city end of Dal Lake, controls the flow of the lake into the Jhelum River canal.

There are two islands in the lake, two real islands anyway, there are other 'sort of' islands joined by causeways. Around the lake are many of Srinagar's most interesting sights, in particular the pleasant Moghul gardens. It's also flanked by hills, particularly along its east bank. The Shankaracharya Hill provides a very fine view over the lake. The waters of Dal Lake are amazingly clear, considering what must get poured into it from the hundreds of houseboats! Nevertheless you're well advised not to go swimming in the lake although the swimming houseboats, equipped with diving boards and chutes, are moored in a deeper part of the lake, 'upstream' from the concentration of houseboats.

There are many tours around the lake but by far the best way to see it is to take a shikara for a day and do a circuit of the Moghul gardens. The cost will be about Rs 50 and there's hardly a lazier and more pleasurable way of getting into the swing of Srinagar. If one of the home-made chocolate merchants comes by and sells you a luxurious quarter kilo of his wares you're set for the day. You can also approach the gardens by road, the Boulevard runs along the eastern edge of the lake, providing fine views all the way.

The lake is probably at its most beautiful when the lotus flowers bloom in July and August. The floating gardens, known as 'rad' in Kashmiri, are one of the stranger aspects of Dal Lake. They're composed of matted vegetation and earth which are cut away from the lake bottom and towed to a convenient location where they are moored. Tomatoes, cucumbers and melons all grow amazingly well in these gardens, if you look underneath you can see that they do literally float on the lake. Of course one problem with a floating garden is that a lazy and dishonest gardener can steal it! You will often see weeds being pulled up out of the lake — this serves a double purpose. The lake waterways are kept clear and the weeds are rotted until they form an excellent compost for the gardens. The shallowness of the lake and it's heavy growth of waterweeds is probably the main reason there are so very few powered boats on the water. Dal Lake would be nowhere near as pleasant if there were powerboats rushing back and forth across its tranquil surface.

Islands
There are three main islands in the lake, each popular excursion points. Silver Island (Sona Lank) is at the northern end of Dal Lake and is also known as Char Chinar after the four (char) chinar trees which grow on it. There's a small snack bar on the island as there is also on Gold Island (Rupa Lank) at the south end of the lake. It is also known as Char Chinar for it too has four chinar trees. The third island is Nehru Park, at the end of the main stretch of the Boulevard and only a short distance from the shore. It too has a restaurant although it's a very run down, miserable affair. North of Nehru Island a long causeway leads out into the lake from the Boulevard. Just off its end is Kotar Khana, the 'house of pigeons', which was once a royal summer house.

The Bund
From above Zero Bridge to below Badshah Bridge you can walk along the banks of the Jhelum River on the popular footpath known as the Bund. It's a pleasant, relaxing place to stroll along and many houseboats can be seen beside it. The GPO, the Government Handicrafts Emporium (in the old British Residency) and a string of handicrafts shops are all close beside the Bund.

Jhelum River & Bridges
The Jhelum flows from Verinag, 80 km south of Srinagar, to the Wular Lake in the north. Passing through Srinagar it's a wide, swift flowing, muddy-looking river. It's famed for its nine old bridges although some of them are

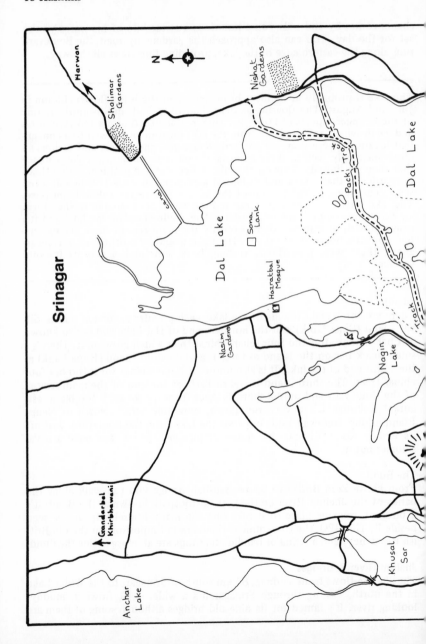

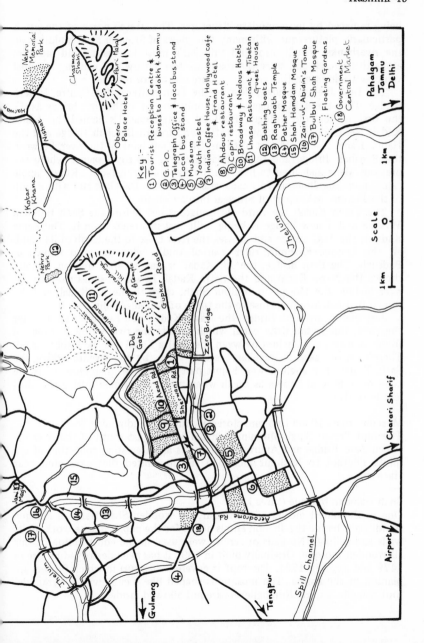

Key:-
1. Tourist Reception Centre & buses to Ladakh & Jammu
2. G.P.O.
3. Telegraph Office & local bus stand
4. Local bus stand
5. Museum
6. Youth Hostel
7. Indian Coffee House, Hollywood cafe & Grand Hotel
8. Ahdous restaurant
9. Capri restaurant
10. Broadway & Nedous Hotels
11. Lhasa Restaurant & Tibetan Guest House
12. Bathing boats
13. Raghunath Temple
14. Pather Mosque
15. Shah Hamdam Mosque
16. Zain-ul-Abidin's Tomb
17. Bulbul Shah Mosque & Floating Gardens
18. Government Central Market

Scale

1 Km   0   1 Km

Pahalgam
Jammu
Delhi

Charari Sharif

Gulmarg

Tengpur

Airport

Spill Channel

Aerodrome Rd

Jhelum

being replaced by more modern structures. The stretch north of the city is particularly picturesque with many fine views of Srinagar's old buildings on the riverbanks. You'll also find Srinagar's most interesting old mosques along this stretch and since the roads are too narrow and winding for most vehicles it's an interesting area to explore on foot or bicycle.

The first Jhelum bridge, close to the Tourist Reception Centre, is Zero Bridge. Thus the next bridge is commonly known as the first bridge as it's the first of the 'old' bridges. Built by Amir Khan it's named the Amira Kadal. Next comes the heavily trafficked modern Badshah Bridge and the Habba Kadal in the old part of town. On the left bank of the river, between the Badshah Bridge and the Habba Kadal, is the royal palace where the previous Maharajah used to live. On the right side the Tsont-i-Kul or 'apple canal' joins the Jhelum. This canal starts from the Dal Gate and with a loop of the Jhelum makes part of Srinagar into an island.

The Fateh Kadal, the third old bridge, is just before the Shah Hamdan Mosque and a new bridge is being built just upstream from it. The Zaina Kadal is the next bridge and crosses the river close to the tomb of its builder, the famous Kashmiri ruler Zain-ul-Abidin who was also known as Badshah. The fifth bridge, the Ali Kadal, is named after his son. Finally there's the Nawa Kadal and the Saffa Kadal. Lesser mosques close to the river include the Mosque of Bulbul Shah, close to the Ali Kadal, and the ruined Badshah Mosque, close to the tomb of Zain-ul-Abidin.

Just below the sixth bridge, the Nawa Kadal, you can see a canal enter the river, this is the Kota canal which diverts the river's flow at times of flood. It leaves the Jhelum between the Amira Kadal and the Habba Kadal. There's an old sarai, a travellers' resting place, by the seventh bridge, the Saffa Kadal. The Jhelum weir is just past this bridge. Also close by is the large open ground known as Idgah where prayers are held during the Moslem Id festival.

Museum (open 10 am to 5 pm, closed Wednesdays, admission free)
The Shri Pratap Singh Museum is in Lal Mandi, just south of the river between Zero Bridge and Amira Kadal. It has an interesting collection of exhibits relevant to Kashmir including the illustrated tiles excavated near Harwan.

Shah Hamdan Mosque (three km)
One of the oldest mosques in Srinagar, the wooden Shah Hamdan Mosque stands right beside the Jhelum and is noted for the papier mache work on its walls and ceilings. No nails or screws were used in the construction of this all wooden mosque. Originally built in 1395 it has been destroyed by fire in 1479 and again in 1731. The roof is covered with turf in which flowers are planted in the spring. The mosque is shaped like a cube with a pyramidal roof rising to a spire. Non-believers are not allowed inside.

Pather Masjid (three km)

Almost directly opposite the Shah Hamdan Mosque, on the other bank of
the Jhelum, the Pather Masjid is a fine stone mosque built by Nur Jahan in
1623. It is not, however, in everyday use today and is consequently rather
run down. Reach it by crossing Zaina Kadal, the fourth bridge.

Tomb of Zain-ul-Abidin (four km)

On the east (right) bank of the river between the Zaina Kadal and the Ali
Kadal is the slightly decrepit tomb of King Zain-ul-Abidin, the highly
regarded son of Sultan Sikander, who built the Jami Masjid. The tomb, built
on the foundations of an earlier temple, shows a clear Persian influence in
its domed construction and glazed tiles.

Jami Masjid (five km)

Srinagar's most important mosque is an impressive wooden structure, notable for the more than 300 soaring pillars supporting the roof, each made of
a single deodar tree trunk. The main gate is to the south and the outer clois-
ters surround a spacious, green and peaceful inner courtyard. The mosque
has had a chequered history — first constructed by Sultan Sikander in 1385,
it was enlarged in 1402 by his son Zain-ul-Abidin but in 1479 it was destroyed by a fire. The mosque was rebuilt by 1503 but was destroyed in another fire during the reign of the Moghul emperor Jehangir. It was rebuilt by
the Kashmiri architect Malik Halder but burnt down yet again in 1674 during the reign of Aurangzeb. The present mosque dates from that time but
was rebuilt, on the last occasion, to the original design.

Shankaracharya Hill

Rising up behind the Boulevard, beside Dal Lake, the hill was once known
as Takht-i-Sulaiman, the Throne of Solomon. It is thought that a temple was
originally built on top of the hill by Jaluka, Ashoka's son, around 200 BC.
The present Hindu temple was built during the reign of the Emperor Jehangir and its enclosing wall and plinth is thought to date from the earlier temple. There's a road running up the hill to the TV transmitting station, just
below the temple, but it's a very pleasant stroll to the top. Go up early, when
the sky is clear, and you'll be rewarded with fine views over the houseboats,
in the lake directly below, and out, across Srinagar to the mountains in the
distance. There are paths leading up from the Nehru Park end of the Boulevard (look for the small pavilion half way up the hill) or from the hospital
at the Tourist Reception Centre end of the Boulevard.

Chasma Shahi (nine km)

Smallest of the Srinagar Moghul gardens, the Chasma Shahi are well up the
hillside, above the Nehru Memorial Park. The fresh water spring in these
pleasant, quieter gardens is reputed to have medicinal properties. The gar-

dens were laid out in 1632 by Ali Mardan Khan. Some extensions have recently been made to the gardens. There is a small shrine, the Chasma Sahibi, near the gardens which also has a fresh water spring.

Pari Mahal (10 km)
The old Sufi college of Pari Mahal is only a short distance above the Chasma Shahi gardens. You can easily walk from the gardens up to the Pari Mahal then follow a footpath directly down the hill to the road that runs by the Oberoi Palace Hotel. The Pari Mahal consists of a series of ruined, arched terraces and had, over the years, become considerably overgrown and neglected. Recently it has been turned into a very pleasant and well kept garden with fine views over Dal Lake from its attractively sited location on a spur of the Zabarwan mountains.

The college was built by Prince Dara Shikah, who had a keen interest in Sufism and Hindu philosophy. The eldest son of Shah Jahan, his right to the throne was usurped by his younger brother who became the Emperor Aurangzeb and was noted for his fanatical Moslem beliefs. There is a shrine to the Goddess Parvati near the foot of the Pari Mahal hill. It's popular on Thursdays in May-June, the Kashmiri month of Jeth.

Nishat Bagh (11 km)
Sandwiched between the lake and the mountains, the Nishat gardens have a particularly fine view across the lake to the Pir Panjal mountain range to the west. The gardens were designed in 1633 by Asaf Khan, brother of Nur Jahan, and follow the same pattern as the Shalimar gardens with a channel running down the centre and a series of terraces. It's the largest of the Moghul gardens and often the most crowded. It has 10 terraces and the remains of some Moghul period buildings.

Shalimar Bagh (15 km)
Set some distance back from the lake, but reached by a small canal, the Shalimar gardens were built by Emperor Jehangir for his wife Nur Jahan, 'light of the world', in 1616. The garden is built in four terraces with the traditional water channel running down the middle. During the Moghul period the top terrace was reserved for the emperor and the ladies of the court and was the most magnificent. It included a pavilion made of black stone in the middle of the tank. The gardens are beautifully kept even today and a son et lumiere (sound and light) show is put on here every evening during the May to October tourist season. The English performance takes place at 9 pm and tickets cost Rs 3 or Rs 7.50. The gardens tend to be very crowded on Sundays.

Hazratbal Mosque (seven km)
If you were doing a clockwise tour of the lake by shikara after winding your way through the floating gardens and the channels and waterways you'd

eventually come out on the open lake and find yourself at the Hazratbal Mosque. The fairly new and shiny mosque, the name means Majestic Palace, enshrines a hair of the prophet but is probably more interesting, to non-Moslems, for its simply stunning situation on the banks of the beautiful lake with the mountains unfolding as a backdrop behind it. The mosque bazaar is fantastically busy on Fridays.

Nasim Bagh (eight km)

Only a short distance beyond the Hazratbal Mosque, the Nasim gardens, the 'gardens of tepid airs', were built by the Moghul Emperor Akbar after his conquest of Kashmir in 1586. He had 1200 chinar trees planted in the garden which is the oldest of Kashmir's Moghul gardens. Today it's used by an engineering college and is not kept up for the public like the other Moghul gardens in Srinagar.

Nagin Lake (eight km)

Known as the 'jewel in the ring', Nagin is generally held to be the most beautiful of the Dal Lakes. Its name comes from the many trees which encircle the small, deep blue lake. Nagin is only separated from the larger Dal Lakes by a narrow causeway and it also has a number of houseboats moored around its perimeter. If you want to really get away from it all then Nagin is a good place to find a houseboat and do it, the surroundings are much more serene and isolated than on Dal Lake. Since the water in Nagin is deeper and less polluted it's also good for swimming and there are fibreglass sailing boats available for hire and water-skiing facilities.

Hari Parbat Fort (five km)

The 18th century fort tops the Sharika hill which is clearly visible, rising to the west of Dal Lake. The fort was constructed by Atta Mohammed Khan but the surrounding wall is much older, it was built between 1592 and 1598 during the rule of Akbar. The wall stretches for five km and is 10 metres high. Visits to the fort are only possible with written permission from the Director of Tourism so for most visitors the fort will remain just a pleasant backdrop. The fort contains a temple revered for its image of the Goddess Sharika. Outside the fort's southern gate there is a shrine to the sixth Sikh Guru. It's known as the Chati Pad Shaki.

Pandrathan Temple (five km)

A small, beautifully proportioned Shiva temple built around 900 AD, the Pandrathan Temple is in the military cantonment area on the Jammu road out of Srinagar.

Harwan (19 km)

Archaeologists have discovered an unusual ornamented brick pavement on the hillside south of this village. You can see examples of the tiles, with their central Asian influence in the peoples' dress and ornaments, in the museum in Srinagar. The water supply for Srinagar is pumped from here and there is a garden and trout hatchery at the site. Harwan is to the north of Dal Lake, four km beyond the Shalimar gardens. The even older archaeological excavations at Burzahom are also near here.

AROUND KASHMIR

There are many interesting places acround the Kashmir Valley. Some of these make good day trips, others are pleasant to stay at in their own right or make good bases for trekking trips or day walks. The J&K Road Transport Corporation operates a variety of day tours around the valley, backed up by privately operated bus company tours. You can also get out and about in local buses or taxis. The two main valley resorts are Pahalgam and Gulmarg. Other places of interest are covered along the route to Pahalgam, the Sindh Valley route, and other places to the south of Srinagar.

ON THE ROAD TO PAHALGAM

The road to Pahalgam starts out towards Jammu but later branches off to the east. There are a number of points of interest along this route including a number of Moghul gardens — indeed if you take a bus tour to Pahalgam you'll be thoroughly saturated with Moghul gardens by the time you arrive.

Pampore (16 km)

Only 16 km out of Srinagar on the main highway south, Pampore is the centre of Kashmir's saffron industry. Highly prized for its flavouring and colouring properties, and rather expensive, saffron is gathered from flowers which are harvested in October.

Sangam (35 km)

A little further down the road, Sangam is interesting for its strong local industry of (amazingly) cricket bat manufacturing! You'll see thousands of cricket bats displayed by the roadside and thousands more roughly cut lengths of wood being seasoned.

Avantipur (29 km)

This popular stop on Pahalgam excursions is noted for its two ruined Hindu temples. The temples were both constructed by King Avantivarman, after whom this ancient centre was named, between 855 and 883 AD. The larger of the two is dedicated to Vishnu and known as the Avantiswami Temple. The central shrine is enclosed by a huge wall with four smaller shrines around the centre. The entrance still bears some fine relief sculptures and the columns have an almost Grecian appearance. The other temple, dedicated to Shiva and known as the Avantishvara, is about a km before the Vishnu temple but also close to the main road. The nearby village of Bijbihara has a huge chinar tree, claimed to be the largest in Kashmir.

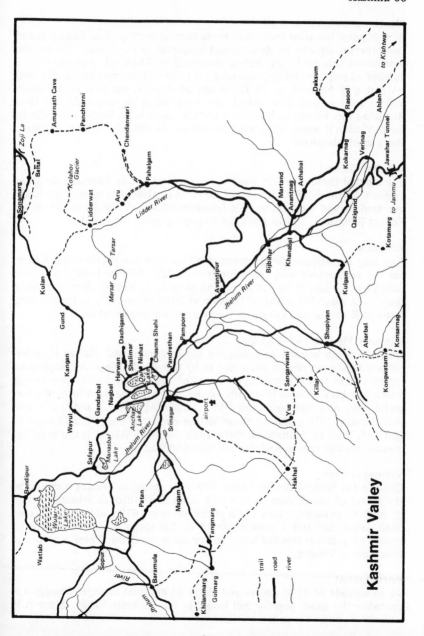

Kashmir Valley

trail
road
river

Anantnag (56 km)
At this point the road forks, one route turning north-east to Pahalgam and two others south-east to Achabal and Kokarnag or to Verinag. The Jammu road leaves this route just before Anantnag at Khanabal. Anantnag has a number of sulphur springs, esteemed for their curative properties. The largest spring is believed to be the home of Ananta, the serpent on which Vishnu reclines and from which the town takes its name. At one time Anantnag was known as Islamabad but this name is no longer used, due to the confusion it would cause with the not too far distant capital of Pakistan, also named Islamabad.

Achabal (58 km)
The Moghul gardens in this small town were laid out by Jahanara, daughter of Shah Jahan, in 1620. It's one of the most carefully designed of the Kashmir gardens and was said to be a favourite retreat of Nur Jahan. There's a Tourist Bungalow, Tourist Huts and a camping ground at Achabal.

Kokarnag
You may be suffering garden overload by the time you get there but Kokarnag has yet another one, noted for its roses. Like Achabal there is a Tourist Bungalow, Tourist Huts and a camping ground. Somewhat above Kokarnag there's the small hill resort of Daksum at 2438 metres. It's on the trekking route to Kishtwar and has a Rest House and Tourist Bungalow.

Mattan & Martand (61 & 64 km)
Only a few km beyond Anantnag, on the Pahalgam road, Mattan is an important Hindu pilgrimage point due to its fish filled springs. A complicated legend relates that the springs were created when Shiva broke open an egg which had been thrown there, the egg being the reincarnated form of a forgetful boy, who had been cursed by a wandering sage ....and that's only half the story! On a plateau above Mattan stands the huge ruined temple of Martand. Built by Lalitaditya Mukhtapida (699-736 AD) it is the most impressive ancient ruin in Kashmir and beautifully sited.

Verinag (80 km)
Close to the foot of the Pir Panjal range, the spring at Verinag is said to be the source of the Jhelum River which flows north through Srinagar. Jehangir built an octagonal stone basin at the spring in 1612 and in 1620 his son, Shah Jahan, laid out a garden around it. The spring is said to be over 15 metres deep and is reputed never to dry up or overflow. There is a Tourist Bungalow at Verinag.

PAHALGAM
At an altitude of 2130 metres and about 95 km from Srinagar, Pahalgam is probably the most popular hill resort in the Kashmir Valley. Since it is

rather lower than Gulmarg the night time temperatures do not drop so low and it has the further advantage of the beautiful Lidder River running right through the town. Pahalgam is situated at the junction of the Lidder and Sheshnag Rivers and surrounded by soaring, fir covered mountains with bare, snow capped peaks rising behind them. There are many short walks available from Pahalgam and in addition it is an excellent base for longer treks such as those to the Kolahoi Glacier or to the Amarnath Cave — see the trekking section for more details. Pahalgam is particularly famed for its many shepherds and they're a common sight, driving their flocks of sheep along the paths all around the town.

Pahalgam Walks
Mamaleswara Only a km or so downstream from Pahalgam, and on the opposite side of the Lidder, this small Shiva temple with its square, stone tank, is thought to date from at least the 12th century, probably earlier.
Baisaran This meadow, about five km above Pahalgam, provides excellent views over the town and the Lidder Valley. If you continue 11 km on beyond Baisaran you reach the Tulian Lake at 3353 metres. It is covered in ice for much of the year.
Aru The pleasant little village of Aru is actually the first stage from Pahalgam on the trek to Lidderwat and the Kolahoi Glacier. It makes an interesting day walk from Pahalgam, following the Lidder River for 11 km upstream. The main track, which also unfortunately takes cars, is on the left bank of the river. There is a less used, and much more difficult, path on the right bank.

Fishing
Kashmir is famous for its trout but they tend to be rather small. Additionally fishing licenses are hard to get and rather expensive. They only allow so many rods on each stretch of the river so there is often a queue for licenses. The cost, in Pahalgam, is Rs 50 per day for the license. Add to that Rs 20 for rod and equipment rental and Rs 20 for the compulsory guide and you've spent Rs 90 before you start — rather a lot for the six fish which is the daily limit. It's not surprising that trout rarely feature on Kashmiri menus!

Accommodation
There is a wide choice of hotels along the main street of Pahalgam and here you will find all the more expensive places. The *Pahalgam Hotel* (tel 26) at Rs 375 for a double room with all meals or the *Woodstock* (tel 27) are probably the top of Pahalgam's hotel list. Other more expensive places are the *Mount View* (tel 21) or the *Natraj Hotel* (tel 25).

There is also a *Government Tourist Bungalow* and *Government Tourist Huts* in Pahalgam and during the summer season the tourist office also operates a number of tent sites with ready set up and furnished tents.

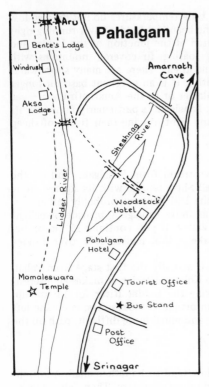

Most western visitors to Pahalgam prefer to stay in one of the lodges across the Lidder River — away from the town itself. Most popular of these lodges is the riverside *Windrush*. There are actually two Windrush Hotels in Pahalgam, which tends to make things a little confusing. The one on the river is sometimes called Windrush II — it's a pleasant place, particularly popular for its warm lounge area where at night you can sit around a pot-bellied stove sampling the large stock of paperbacks. Costs can get down to as low as Rs 10 before the height of the season but Rs 40 for a double is more likely to be the cost during the season. Fairly good food, excellent breakfasts (on the verandah looking out over the river) and good desserts.

Up the hill, a little beyond Windrush, is the rather cheaper and rather more basic *Bente's Hotel* with singles as low as Rs 7, doubles around Rs 20. It's also popular with western visitors. Finally there's the *Aksa Lodge* which is also slightly up the hill, just before Windrush. It's rather flashier and more luxurious (even running hot water) but not so friendly. Doubles here start from around Rs 50 and go up to Rs 100 or more. Take care when enquiring what you get or you'll end up being charged extra for a blanket on the bed! Nice views from the verandah over the valley. If you want to camp, with your own camping equipment, any of these 'across the river' places will probably be good places to enquire.

At Aru there's a *Government Tourist Hut*, small tea houses where you could probably get shelter and the *Greenview Guest House*, down by the river, a little before the town. There are also rumours of a new de-luxe hotel being built in Aru and the road to Aru being upgraded for the expected 5-star visitors — pray that it doesn't happen.

Getting to Pahalgam
Local buses cost Rs 4.50 and take 2½ to four hours, there are six to 10 departures a day. J&K Road Transport have tour buses which cost Rs 10 one way or Rs 20 return. The KMDA tour buses take a long time since they make many stops on the way. Taxis cost over Rs 200 return although you can sometimes find a taxi going back from Pahalgam empty and willing to bargain. If you want to get a return ticket on one of the more comfortable J&K tour buses you have to catch them when they come in around noon in order to get tickets. Get someone from your hotel to do it for you. Ponies can easily be hired in Pahalgam for trekking trips. The fixed costs to popular destinations are all clearly posted.

Information
The tourist office (tel 24) is just around the corner from the bus halt, on the main road. They may be able to help with hiring porters or ponies but otherwise are not much use. Fishing permits have to be obtained in Srinagar. There is a bank in Pahalgam and a post office. If you're planning on trekking from Pahalgam there are plenty of shops selling food supplies.

GULMARG
The valley of Gulmarg, a large meadow about three square km in area, stands at 2730 metres, 52 km from Srinagar. The name means 'meadow of flowers' and in the spring it's just that, a rolling meadow dotted with countless colourful flowers. It's a popular day trip from Srinagar although many people extend their stay or use it as a base for trekking. Note that it can be much colder than down in Srinagar, sleeping bags are essential. In the winter Gulmarg is the skiing centre of India, there are four ski-lifts on the slopes. In summer it boasts one of the highest altitude golf courses in the world. There are many huts and hotels scattered around the flower covered fields.

Gulmarg Walks
Outer Circular Walk A circular road, 11 km in length, runs right round Gulmarg through pleasant pine forests with excellent views over the Kashmir Valley. Nanga Parbat is visible to the north and Haramukh and Sunset Peak to the south-east.
Khilanmarg This smaller valley is about a six km walk from the Gulmarg bus stop and car park. The meadow, carpeted with flowers in the spring, is the site for Gulmarg's winter ski-runs and offers a fine view of the surround-

ing peaks and over the Kashmir Valley. During the early spring, as the snow melts, it can be a very muddy hour's climb up the hill.

Alpather Beyond Khilanmarg, 13 km from Gulmarg at the foot of the 4511 metre Apharwat peak, this lake is frozen until mid-June and even later in the year you can see lumps of ice floating in its cold waters. The walk from Gulmarg follows a well graded pony track over the 3810 metre Apharwat Ridge, separating it from Khilanmarg, and then up the valley to the lake at 3843 metres.

Ningle Nallah Flowing from the melting snow and ice on Apharwat and the Alpather Lake, this pretty mountain stream is 10 km from Gulmarg. The stream continues down into the valley below and joins the Jhelum River near Sopore. The walking path crosses the Ningle Nallah by a bridge and continues on to the Lienmarg, another grassy meadow and a good spot for camping.

Ferozpore Nallah Reached from the Tangmarg road, or from the outer circular walk, this mountain stream meets the Bahan River at a popular picnic spot known as 'waters meet'. The stream is reputed to be particularly good for trout fishing; it's about five km from Gulmarg. You can continue on from here to Tosamaidan, a three day, 50 km walk to one of Kashmir's most beautiful margs.

Ziarat of Baba Reshi This Moslem shrine is on the slopes below Gulmarg and can be reached from either Gulmarg or Tangmarg. The Ziarat, or tomb, is of a well known Moslem saint who died here in 1480. Before renouncing worldly ways he was a courtier of the Kashmir king Zain-ul-Abidin.

Accommodation

Gulmarg has a couple of up-market hotels and a number at the other end of the scale. *Nedou's* (tel 28) is open only from May to October and costs from Rs 250 for a double, room only. *Hotel Highland Park* (tel 30 & 34) is a bit more expensive but even if you're a shoestring traveller it's worth a visit for a cup of tea or coffee in the beautiful gardens (or even a beer in a crested silver tankard!). It's a rather fine establishment.

The cheaper hotels include the *City View* and *Mount View* at around Rs 20 a double — OK but spartan, you really need a fire in the spring or autumn and wood is extra. It's worth remembering how much colder Gulmarg is than Srinagar. The *New Punjabi Hotel*, opposite the Gundwara, is also very cheap. *Kingsley's* (tel 55) is a big, rambling old place with doubles from around Rs 100. It also has a fairly good, but slightly pricey, restaurant.

Getting to Gulmarg

There are a variety of buses running from Srinagar to Gulmarg, many of them on day tours. On a day tour you have only a few hours at the hill resort, just long enough for one of the shorter day walks. The de-luxe tour buses cost Rs 21 return or Rs 11 one-way and leave at 9 am from the Tourist Reception Centre. Ordinary buses leave hourly and cost Rs 10 return or

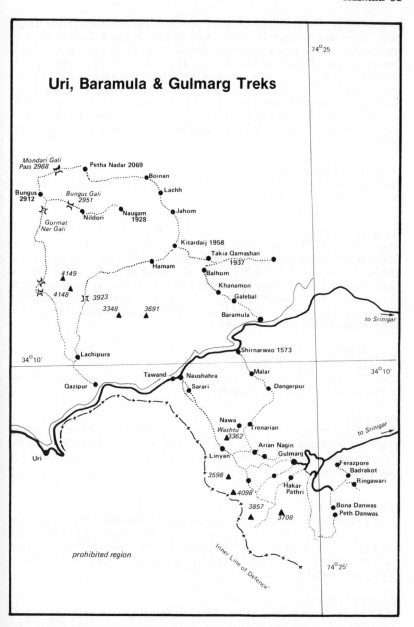

Uri, Baramula & Gulmarg Treks

Mondari Gali Pass 2968
Petha Nadar 2069
Boinan
Lachh
Bungus 2912
Bungus Gali 2951
Jahom
Gormat Nar Gali
Nildori
Naugam 1928
Kitardaij 1958
Takia Qamashan 1937
Hamam
Balhom
Khanamon
Galebal
▲ 4149
▲ 4148
〕 3923
Baramula
to Srinigar
▲ 3348
▲ 3691
Lachipura
Shirnarwao 1573
34° 10'
34° 10'
Tawand
Naushahra
Malar
Qazipur
Sarari
Dangerpur
Nawa Washtu 3362
Trenarian
Arian Nagin
to Srinigar
Linyan
Gulmarg
Uri
Ferazpore
Badrakot
▲ 3598
Ringawari
▲ 4098
Hakar Pathri
▲ 3857
3708
Bona Danwas
Peth Danwas
prohibited region
Inner Line of Defence
74° 25'
74° 25'

Rs 6 one-way. Until recently the road from Srinagar only ran as far as Tang-marg, seven km distance or 500 metres altitude below Gulmarg. The last stretch then had to be completed on foot or by pony. A road has now been completed over the last stretch although there are still buses operating that terminate at Tangmarg. The winding road from Tangmarg is 13 km in length, nearly twice as far as the more direct pony track. A riding pony costs Rs 12 from Tangmarg up to Gulmarg. Ponies, either riding or pack ponies, can also be hired from Gulmarg to other sites around the valley. Khilanmarg, for example, costs Rs 20 return. Other rates are prominently posted at the car park.

SOUTH OF SRINAGAR
There are several other interesting places south of Srinagar, principally to the south-west of the valley.

Yusmarg (40 km)
Standing in the Pir Panjal hills, out beyond the airport, at an altitude of 2700 metres, the meadow of Yusmarg is reputed to have the best spring flowers in Kashmir. Near to Yusmarg is the picturesque Nila Nag lake where there is a Forest Rest House. Yusmarg has Tourist Huts and is a good base for treks into the surrounding hills. Popular treks include those to Sangisafaid (Chitta Pathar), Dodha Patri or to Sunset Peak — the highest mountain in the Pir Panjal range at 4746 metres.

Chari Sharif (30 km)
Situated on the road to Yusmarg, this is the site of the shrine or Ziarat of Sheik Noor-ud-Din, the patron saint of Kashmir. The valley also has the ziarats of a number of his followers.

Aharbal
This was another popular resting place for the Moghul emperors when they made the long trip north from Delhi to Kashmir. It's in an area famed for its apples and also has an interesting waterfall. It's also the start of the popular trek to the Konsarnag Lake.

SINDH VALLEY
North of Srinagar the Sindh Valley is an area of mountains, lakes, rivers and glaciers. The Sindh River flows down from the Amarnath and Harmukh glaciers into the Anchar Lake. The Leh road from Srinagar follows this river to beyond Sonamarg. The Zoji La Pass marks the boundary from the Sindh Valley into Ladakh.

Dachigam (21 km)
This wildlife reserve was, at one time, the royal game reserve but animals

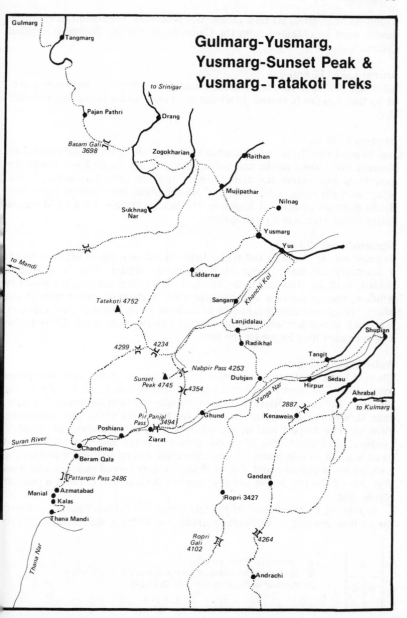

**Gulmarg-Yusmarg,
Yusmarg-Sunset Peak &
Yusmarg-Tatakoti Treks**

within its boundaries are now completely protected. Permission to enter the reserve must be obtained from the Game Warden at the Tourist Reception Centre.

Anchar Lake (11 km)
Although this large lake is no great distance from Srinagar and easily reached by bus, it is rarely visited. In winter it is home for a wide variety of water birds.

Gandarbal (19 km)
Just beyond the Wular and Manasbal Lakes turn-off from the Leh road, this pleasant little town marks the point where the icy Sindh River leaves the mountains and enters the plains. About five km from Gandarbal, in the village of Tullamulla, is the shrine of Khirbhawani, the Goddess Ragni, the Hindu guardian goddess of Kashmir. The marble temple, built by Maharaja Pratap Singh, stands in a small spring.

Manasbal Lake (28 km)
Situated on the route to the Wular Lake via Safapur, this clear, deep lake is a sanctuary for many water birds during the winter. There is a Moghul garden, built by Nur Jahan, by the lake. It's called Garoka, meaning bay window, due to its view out over the lake. A grove of chinar trees at the nearby village of Safapur is known as Badshah Boni, Royal Chinar. Camping is possible at another lakeside chinar grove known as Qoz Bagh. There is also a Government Rest House by the lake.

Wular Lake (50 km)
Claimed to be the largest freshwater lake in Asia, the Wular Lake can spread over nearly 200 square km but its actual surface area tends to vary during the year. The Jhelum River flows into the lake and then out again. The lake, calm though it may appear, is noted for the fierce winds that sometimes blow up. The deepest part of the lake is known as Mota Khon, the 'Gulf of Corpses', since the bodies of people drowned in the lake were all supposed to be washed to this place. At one time there was an artificial island on the lake, where boatmen could shelter if the weather turned bad, but silting on that side of the lake has joined the island to the lakeside. It's now a popular picnic spot.

Sopore, at the south end of the lake where the Jhelum leaves it, is noted for its fruit growing — particularly apples and walnuts. Baramula, a little to

A Jhelum River in Srinagar
B Shah Hamdan Mosque, on the Jhelum River, Srinagar
C Pari Mahal, looking out over Dal Lake

the south-west, was on the main route to Rawalpindi, the chief route from Kashmir to the Indian plains prior to independence. Baramula is the legendary place from which Vishnu is said to have drained the waters which once filled the Kashmir Valley. The lake can be reached by river as well as road. Close to Shadipore, where the Sindh River flows into the Jhelum, there are the ruins of a number of Hindu and Buddhist shrines. Shadipore has a camping site and is noted for the abundant fish in the waters around it. Narmarg, above the lake, is a popular trekking centre.

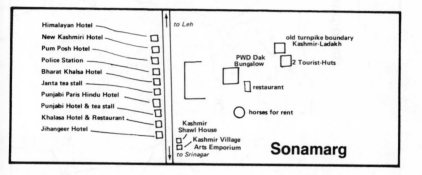

Sonamarg (83 km)

At a height of 2740 metres, Sonamarg is the last major point in the Kashmir Valley before the Zoji La pass into Ladakh. At the pass the green, lush Kashmiri landscape abruptly switches to the barren, dry landscape of Ladakh. Sonamarg is thus not only a good base for treks but also a jumping off point for trips into Ladakh. The name means 'Meadow of Gold' and although this could be due to the profusion of flowers that carpet the meadow in the spring it is also possible that the name derives from Sonamarg's strategic trading position in the days when this was a major route into central Asia. One of the most popular short walks from Sonamarg is the four km route to Thajiwas, a small valley at the foot of the Sonamarg glacier. A path leads up to the Shakhdar Hill, overlooking the glacier from the north-east. There are Tourist Huts, a Rest House and some small hotels at Sonamarg. The Rest House is exactly midway between Sonamarg and Thajiwas.

A Shikaras, assembled at a ghat on Dal Lake
B Vegetable shikara on a Srinagar canal
C Nishat Bagh by Dal Lake

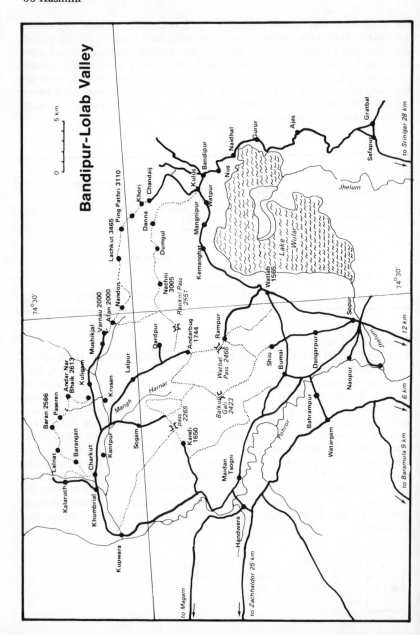

Bandipur-Lolab Valley

Baltal (98 km)
This small village is right at the foot of the Zoji La pass and thus is the final village in Kashmir. It stands at a height of 2743 metres and has a Rest House and camping ground. It is possible to walk to the Amarnath Cave, more usually approached from Pahalgam, and back to Baltal in one day — but only during the month of June. Prior to that the weather can be treacherous and after June the melting snow and ice make the route very dangerous. A number of snow bridges have to be crossed and when the ice starts to melt these soon become unsafe.

SONAMARG-WANGAT
This 81 km trek takes six days and reaches a maximum altitude of 4191 metres.

Day 1: Srinagar-Sonamarg
The 84 km journey from Srinagar to Sonamarg takes three to four hours by bus or car. The route goes though the villages of Ganderbal, Gund and Kalan en route to Sonamarg which is the last large village in the Kashmir Valley on the way to Leh. Sonamarg is at an altitude of 2720 metres and has tourist huts as well as wood and water if you are camping. Ponies can be rented in Sonamarg.

Day 2: Sonamarg-Nichinai
Half a kilometre past the Shitkari bridge the trail leaves the bank of the Sindh and climbs up the left side of the mountain. Nichinai is at 3620 metres, 910 metres above Sonamarg and 15 km distance. Wood and water are on hand in the camp.

Day 3: Nichinai-Krishansar
The 13 km trek starts by crossing the 4080 metres Nichinai chain then follows the river before crossing it at Hirampathri. You pass by Vishansar at 3680 metres and reach the camp at Krishansar at 3819 metres. There is a good site for camping with water available and trout fishing possibilities but the only wood is that sold by nomads at rather high prices.

Day 4: Krishansar-Dubta Pani
You cross the Razbal Gali at 4191 metres and follow the right bank of the river. The route descends to the Gadsar Lake at 3680 metres and crosses the river at Gadsar Maidan. There is no wood at Dubta Pani, you should collect fuel on the final ascent to the camp at 3280 metres.

Day 5: Dubta Pani-Gangabal Lake
The day's 17 km trek starts with an ascent to the Satsaran Gali pass at 3680 metres, it's only open from June to October. You have a fine view of the Satsar Lake at 3600 metres. The climb then follows to the 4081 metres

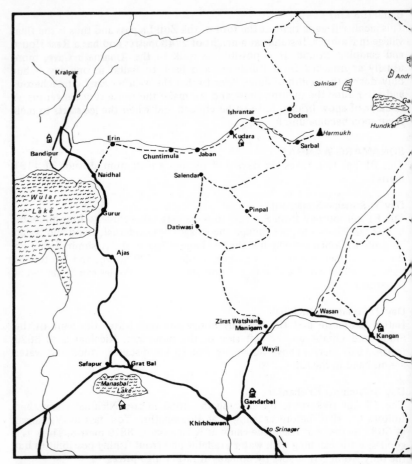

Zajibal Gali pass, also open only from June to October. From here you can
see the Nund Kol Lake at 3501 metres. The camp site at Gangabal Lake
(3570 metres) has wood, water and trout fishing. The lake, at the foot of
Harmukh, is the site for a major pilgrimage each August.

Day 6: Gangabal Lake-Wangat
The 19 km trek descends 1500 metres to Wangat at 2050 metres. There is a
Rest House as well as camping facilities, with wood and water, at Wangat.
About five km from Wangat there are the interesting ruins of two old tem-
ples. It's possible to get back to Srinagar from Wangat on the same day,
about 2½ hours by road.

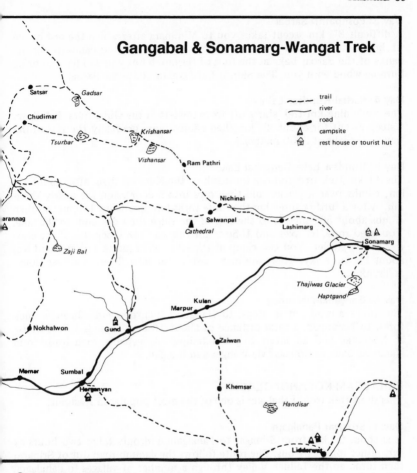

Gangabal & Sonamarg-Wangat Trek

GANGABAL TREK (via Poshpathri)
Day 1: Srinagar-Erin
It is about 80 km from Srinagar to Erin via Bandipur. There is a Rest House and riverbank camping sites at Erin which stands at 1983 metres.

Day 2: Erin-Chuntimula-Poshpathri
The 11 km trek starts by crossing the Erin River near the Rest House. The first three or four km of the route, which ascends in stages, is in good condition as it is maintained by the forest small-holders. The route passes the village of Kudara, where there is a Rest House, and reaches Poshpathri at 2440 metres.

Day 3: Poshpathri-Sarbal

A difficult 8½ km ascent takes you to Minimarg after which the rest of the 11 km route to Sarbal is not so difficult. There is a good campsite on the banks of the Sarbal Lake at the foot of Harmukh but you will have to bring burning wood with you. The Shirsar Lake stands above the Sarbal.

Day 4: Sarbal-Kundsar Lake

The day's nine km trek starts off from the left of the Gujar huts. It follows a steep ascent for about 2½ km then climbs more gradually the rest of the way to the lake at 3800 metres.

Day 5: Kundsar Lake-Gangabal Lake

The 11 km trek first follows the bank of the Kundsar then, after about 1½ km, climbs over a glacier and then dips into a depression for nearly three km. After a further three km the route turns left and drops 150 metres then climbs about 500 metres to the top of the ridge then descends to the lake. You need rope, ice-axes and U-bolts for this day's trek because of the crevices in the glacier. You can camp at the lake (3572 metres) or at Nund Kol about 1½ km away. There are many fish in the lake. There is a Rest House at Trunkul.

Day 6: Gangabal-Narannag

The route ascends, with steps, to Harigund then descends through thick forest to Narannag, a total distance of about 16 km. There is a Rest House at Narannag and an interesting old temple. A jeepable road leads from Narannag back to Srinagar via Wangat and Kangan.

PAHALGAM-KOLAHOI GLACIER

This short trek from Pahalgam is one of the most popular in Kashmir.

Day 1: Srinagar-Pahalgam

It is about 90 km from Srinagar to Pahalgam and only takes two hours by car, rather longer by bus. The route follows the Jammu road out of Srinagar then turns up the Lidder Valley through a number of villages to Pahalgam. There are fine views of rice paddies and snow capped peaks all along the road. The Lidder has many fish but a trout fishing licence is rather expensive. Pahalgam is at 2130 metres and has a wide variety of accommodation.

Day 2: Pahalgam-Aru

It is only about 12 km from Pahalgam (the 'village of shepherds') to Aru and cars can also follow this part of the route, which runs along the right bank of the Lidder River through pine forest. Riding and load carrying ponies can easily be obtained in Pahalgam either directly from the pony owners or through the Tourist Office. Aru is a picturesque little village at the confluence of two smaller rivers. The PWD Rest House in Aru has two rooms

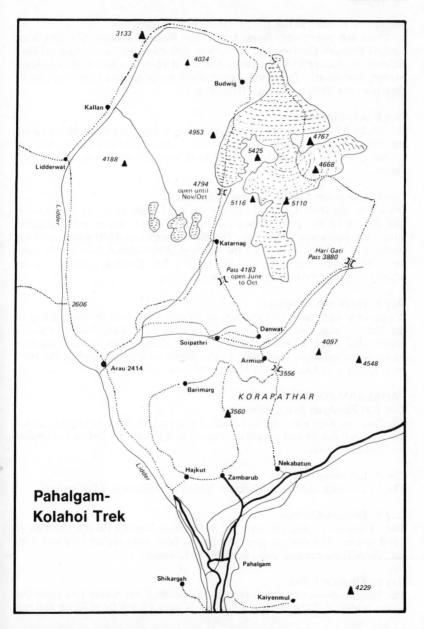

Pahalgam-Kolahoi Trek

and can be booked at the Tourist Office in Pahalgam.

There are two routes from Aru to the Kolahoi Glacier. The first leads straight through the forest to Lidderwat and starts with a steep ascent then follows the Lidder River for the rest of the stretch. The other route is much harder, particularly for ponies, and goes right to Armiun (past Soipathri) then over the 3880 metre high Harigati pass.

Day 3: Aru-Lidderwat
It is about 12 km from Aru to Lidderwat where there is a magnificent camping location at the meeting point of the Kolahoi Glacier's stream and the stream from the Tarwar Lake. Lidderwat also has a two-room PWD Rest House.

Day 4: Lidderwat-Kolahoi Glacier-Lidderwat
It's a day trip from Lidderwat to the glacier (13 km) or to the Tarsar Lake. The stretch to the glacier leads east through a pine forest until Satlanjan where the landscape opens out. The glacier begins at 3400 metres and extends to over 4000 metres. To the north-west of Kolahoi, beneath the glacier, is the Dudh Nag Lake at 4267 metres. The Kolahoi mountain, from which the glacier descends, is 5485 metres high.

Day 5: Lidderwat-Pahalgam
It's an easy walk back to Pahalgam or an extra day may be spent going to the Tarsar Lake. From the lake at 3962 metres you can climb over a 250 metre ridge which separates Tarsar from the Marsar Lake. It is also possible to continue on from Lidderwat to the Sindh Valley, intersecting the road from Srinagar to Leh near Sonamarg. This trek is detailed below:

PAHALGAM-SONAMARG TREK
Day 1-2: Pahalgam-Aru-Lidderwat
The first two days are as for the Kolahoi Glacier trek from Pahalgam. An additional day can be added here to actually visit the glacier before continuing on from Lidderwat.

Day 3: Lidderwat-Sekiwas
The 10 km walk ascends the Sekiwas Nallah to Sekiwas at 3430 metres.

Day 4: Sekiwas-Khemsar
The 11 km trek takes you over the 4115 metre Yemhar Pass to Khemsar at 3659 metres. The descent from the pass is fairly easy during July and August. There is no burning wood available at Khemsar.

Day 5: Khemsar-Kulan
The trail descends through forests to the Sindh River where you cross the Kulan bridge at 2226 metres. Sonamarg is only 16 km from Kulan and can

be reached either by a good track up the Sindh Valley or by bus.

PAHALGAM-AMARNATH CAVE
At the time of the full moon in the month of Shravan (July-August) thousands of Hindu pilgrims make the annual 'Yatra' to the Shri Amarnath Cave. Situated at 3900 metres, 45 km from Pahalgam, the cave contains a natural ice lingam, the symbol of Lord Shiva. During the Yatra it is possible to obtain wood, kerosene and other necessities at Chandanwari, Sheshnag and Panchtarni but at other times these must be brought from Pahalgam.

Day 1: Pahalgam-Chandanwari
The route follows a jeepable road for 13 km to Chandanwari at 2900 metres. There is a PWD Rest House at Chandanwari where the Sheshnag and Astanmarg rivers meet. Chandanwari is famous for its snow bridge.

Day 2: Chandanwari-Sheshnag
There is a choice of routes for this 12 km trek. One goes past the Pisu Hill while the other goes via the Pisu ghati, this is the pilgrim route. The Sheshnag Lake is at 3700 metres and there are camping facilities at Zojipal or a small PWD hut at Wavjan.

Day 3: Sheshnag-Panchtarni
It is 11 km from Sheshnag to Panchtarni where again there is a small PWD hut as well as, in season, sheds for the pilgrims. It is possible to walk from Chandanwari to Panchtarni in one day. Panchtarni means 'five streams' since it is the meeting point of five small rivers.

Day 4: Panchtarni-Amarnath Cave
The final stretch to the cave is just eight km. It is possible to continue from the Amarnath Cave to Baltal, on the Srinagar-Leh road about 13 km from Sonamarg. This is a possible alternative to returning from the cave to Pahalgam.

PAHALGAM-PANNIKAR TREK (Suru Valley)
This is quite a hard trek best made between June and September. Porters can be hired in Pahalgam but you must reckon on Rs 40 or more per day. You should carry a tent and all necessities must be brought from Pahalgam including food and kerosene for cooking. The only place with lodging available is Chandanwari and Sheshnag, as on the Amarnath Cave trek.

Day 1 & Day 2: Pahalgam-Chandnwari-Sheshnag
As on Amarnath Cave trek.

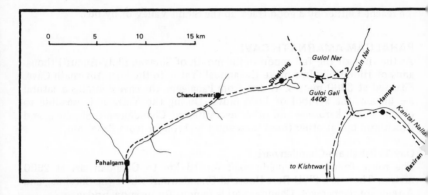

Day 3: Sheshnag-Rangmarg
The route ascends the 4406 metre Gulol Gali Pass then descends on the left bank of the Gulol Nar down to the mouth of the Sain Nar. Here you take the right bank (definitely not the left!) and complete the 7.5 km walk to Rangmarg.

Day 4: Rangmarg-Hampet
The trail follows the Sain Nar until it joins the Kanital Nallah on the left then follows on the left bank to Hampet, a total distance of 5.5 km.

Day 5 & 6: Hampet-foot of the Lonvilad Gali
From Hampet the track continues on the left bank of the Kanital Nallah to Baziran. Here the route divides with a long route leading straight ahead to Pannikar. You follow the Kanital on its right bank to the foot of the Lonvilad Gali, a total distance of 22 km over the two days.

Day 7: Lonvilad Gali
The 4660 metre high Lonvilad Gali has to be ascended and the descent is then made over a glacier which comes from the Chalong Nallah. The overnight halt is made at the foot of the glacier.

Day 8: Chalong Glacier-Pannikar
The 15 km walk starts with the descent into the valley of the Chalong Nallah which is then followed to Pannikar. From Pannikar there is a road leading north to Kargil or east to the Zanskar Valley.

KONSARNAG TREK (Pir Panjal Range)
This four or five day trek reaches a maximum altitude of 3700 metres.

Day 1: Srinagar-Ahrabal
It takes three to four hours to reach Ahrabal by road from Srinagar. The

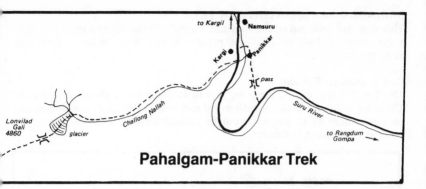

to Kargil

Namsuru

Kargil

Panikkar

pass

Suru River

Lonvilad
Gali
4860

glacier

Challong Nallah

to Rangdum
Gompa

Pahalgam-Panikkar Trek

journey leads through a number of picturesque villages standing in the rice paddies. On the last part of this stretch the road ascends gradually. There is a government Rest House and a good camping site (with water and wood) at Ahrabal. The waterfall, about 10 km from Ahrabal, and the conifer forest past the Rest House are of interest. Ahrabal is at 2460 metres.

Day 2: Ahrabal-Kungwattan
The nine km trek to Kungwattan only takes about three hours. The route follows the Vishav River to the 1½ square km Kungwattan meadow at 2559 metres. There is a Rest House at Kungwattan with two rooms. With an early start from Srinagar you can reach Kungwattan on the first day.

Day 3: Kungwattan-Mahinag
The day's walk starts through thick forest then climbs slowly beside the Vishav River. The plateau of Mahinag is surrounded by lovely mountains and has a group of glass-clear, ice-cold springs. Mountaineers can find a number of climbing opportunities in this area. It is possible to continue straight on to the mountain lake of Konsarnag in the same day but it is better to camp for the night at Mahinag which is at 2989 metres.

Day 4: Mahinag-Konsarnag-Kungwattan
The two km long Konsarnag Lake is situated in a beautiful high dale at 3700 metres. The deep, dark blue waters are excellent for swimming and there are good climbing opportunities to the north-east. It is recommended that you return straight to Kungwattan in the same day.

Day 5: Kungwattan-Srinagar
From Kungwattan you return to Ahrabal and then to Srinagar by road.

SRINAGAR-DAKSUM-KISHTWAR TREK
This five day trek out of the Kashmir Valley into the Jammu region reaches a maximum altitude of 3700 metres and is best made between June and September.

Day 1: Srinagar-Daksum
The 100 km trip can be made by bus or taxi and takes about three hours. There are camping facilities with wood and water in Daksum and ponies can be hired there or in Wagil. Overnight accommodation in Daksum must be booked beforehand in Srinagar.

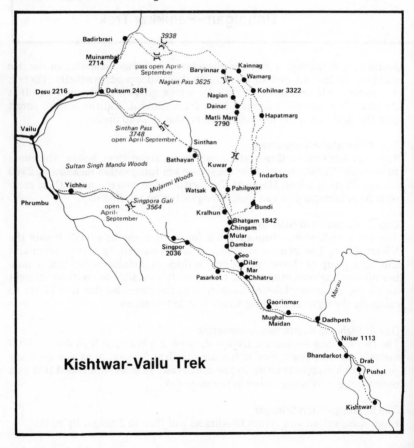

Day 2: Daksum-Sinthan Pass
This 16 km trek takes about five to six hours and reaches the maximum altitude of the trek. There are wooden huts in Sinthan and wood and water are on hand.

Day 3: Sinthan-Chatru
The day's eight km trek only takes two or three hours. Wood and water are available at the camping area and there is a small shop for replenishing provisions in the village.

Day 4: Chatru-Mughal Maidan
There are again some shops in the village which is reached after a nine km trek.

Day 5: Mughal Maidan-Dadpath
There are daily buses at 10 am and 4 pm from Dadpath to Kishtwar. Dadpath is only eight km from Mughal Maidan. Kishtwar has a Dak Bungalow and other accommodation or camping possibilities. Kishtwar has some notable waterfalls and is also a centre of saffron cultivation. It's a popular jumping off point for other treks (including one into Zanskar) and mountain climbing. From Kishtwar you can reach either Jammu or Srinagar by bus in one day.

Ladakh

It has been called 'the moonland', 'little Tibet' or 'the last Shangri La'. Those romantic definitions all hold more than a slight degree of truth. Ladakh is the most remote region of India, a barren, virtually rainless area which lies north of the Himalayas, an area known geographically as the Tibetan plateau. The Himalayas serve as a barrier to clouds carrying rain from the south, virtually none of it gets across to fall on Ladakh which, in consequence, has only a few cm of rain per year. As little as the Sahara. The result is the 'moonland' label — much of Ladakh looks much like the moon, a barren, grey-brown landscape utterly devoid of vegetation. Only where rivers, running from far-away glaciers or melting snow, carry water to habitation do you find plant life.

Ladakh really is a 'little Tibet'. Although Tibet is politically part of China today, Ladakh, like parts of Nepal, is situated on the Tibetan plateau. The people of Ladakh are related to the Tibetans and follow similar cultural and religious practices. Ladakh also has many Tibetan refugees who fled Tibet with the invasion from China. Ladakh today is probably far more Tibetan than Tibet itself, where the Tibetan culture has, no doubt, been considerably changed by the Chinese.

Finally Ladakh could well be 'the last Shangri La'. Due to its strategic location — the area is disputed by the Indians, Pakistanis and Chinese — it has been virtually closed to outsiders from the end of WW II right up to 1974. The daunting height of the Himalayas added to this isolation, even today the main route into Ladakh is only open for six months of each year. Until 1979 there was no regular civilian flight into Ladakh so from October to June the region was completely cut off.

Today Ladakh is open to outsiders, or at least as open as its geography permits. No special permission is needed to enter Ladakh and within the region you can travel around with relative freedom. Ladakh is full of amazing sights — strange gompas perched on soaring hilltops, dwarfed by snow-capped mountains; the barren, shattered looking landscapes splashed with small but brilliant patches of green; ancient palaces clinging to sheer rock walls. But most of all it is notable for its delightful people — friendly as only Tibetans can be and immensely colourful. It's an amazing place.

HISTORY

Until the 10th century Ladakh was regarded as a province of Tibet, where Buddhism was the dominant religion. With the collapse of the Tibetan empire the border regions became independent kingdoms under local rulers. At that time Ladakh was conquered by Palgyi-Gon, who came from the Tibetan royal family. From then until the 16th century little of interest occurred until Chovang Namgyal, also a descendant of the kings of Tibet and a native of Lhasa, conquered Ladakh in 1533. At this time Jehangir was the Moghul ruler of India but the Namgyal dynasty of Ladakh exists even

78

today — the Rani of Stok still occupies the Stok palace and has been elected to the Indian parliament.

The first Namgyal king extended the region under Ladakhi control and received tribute from the Nubra Valley but his descendant was defeated in a war with the Moslem king of Balti, who laid waste to all the monasteries in Ladakh. A generation later another invasion from Balti was supported by the Moghul emperor but King Singe Namgyal defeated them. Encouraged by this success and subsequent conquests of neighbouring kingdoms he then planned an attack on Lhasa but was dissuaded by the receipt of gifts from Tibet. These events occurred shortly after the conquest of Tibet by the great lama Navang Lozang in 1640.

Singe Namgyal divided the kingdom between his three sons. His descendant in Ladakh, Deldan Namgyal, had the golden Buddha statue erected in Shey and his generals subjugated the Baltis and made them pay tribute. Kashmiri troops, assisting the Baltis, were also beaten by the Ladakhis but in the following years (around 1685) the Ladakhis were unable to repel invading Mongol forces. Ladakh once again came under Tibetan influence and in order to escape this domination the Ladakhis sought and received military support from their former enemies, the Kashmiris. The Governor of Kashmir sent troops to help the King of Leh regain his throne, but in return for this help the king had to pay a regular tribute to Delhi and a mosque had

monk at Mulbekh

to be erected in Leh. Some sources maintain that the king actually had to convert to Islam but this is uncertain.

In the following years, until it was completely conquered by Kashmir, Ladakh was ruled by insignificant kings. After the establishment of Sikh rule over Jammu and Kashmir, Ladakh was conquered by the Wezir Zorawar Singh, the general of Maharajah Gulab Singh. This event is known as the Dogra Invasion of 1834. The palace of Leh was devastated and a fortification built south of the town — it's a military camp today. The King of Ladakh was dethroned and his place taken by various town governors appointed by the Maharajah of Jammu, who was descended from Ladakhi nobility (Chalons). Thus only the military was comprised of Kashmiris, the government was again in Ladakhi hands. The dethroned royal family received Stok, the palace where they still live today. The last king, Kunsang Namgyal, died in 1974 but is expected to be succeeded by his son when he reaches an appropriate age.

Since India's independence, and the resulting conflict between India and Pakistan over Kashmir, Ladakh, like Kashmir, has been divided between the two nations. Following the Chinese invasion of Tibet in 1959 there have been Indian and Chinese troops stationed on the eastern border and in 1962 there was another major conflict when the Chinese occupied part of Ladakh including the Changchenmo Valley. Since then Ladakh has been divided into three parts. Due to the strong military presence in Ladakh India has considerably developed the region's infrastructure but the Chinese and Pakistanis have also been hard at work, building strategically important roads. There is now a road through the Chinese held part of Ladakh, close to the ceasefire line, it links Lhasa, the capital of Tibet, over the Karakorum range into the Pakistani region and the Indus Valley, west of Kargil.

GENERAL ADVICE

Take a sleeping bag with you, even in summer it can get very chilly at night and if you spend the night at a monastery or village you'll definitely need warm bedding. If you use public transport from Leh there are gompas which can only be visited if you stay overnight and return the next day — due to the bus timings. If you're planning to do much travelling around Ladakh a tent is also worth having, for similar reasons. If you're trekking it's a necessity.

Be prepared for dramatic changes in temperatures and watch out for the sun's surprising intensity at this altitude. On a warm day the temperature can drop with striking speed when a cloud obscures the sun. You will find yourself putting on and taking off a sweater a dozen times a day. The burning power of the sun in Ladakh is phenomenal, if you want to avoid sunburn and a peeling nose you'll find a sun screen cream is essential. A hat also helps.

Remember the effects of altitude — people who fly straight to Leh from Delhi should take it very easy for a few days until they're acclimatised.

Even from Srinagar at 1768 metres you're likely to feel breathless and light headed at Leh's 3554 metres. Take it easy, don't over-exert yourself at first. Bad headaches and nausea are common effects of lack of acclimatisation, they're particularly prevalent at night. Severe altitude sickness, which can be fatal, is extremely unlikely to afflict you unless you immediately start rushing up mountains. There's only one sure treatment for altitude sickness and that is to get down to a lower level. People with heart conditions should seek medical advice before visiting Ladakh — your heart has to work hard at this height. Remember that the effects of alcohol are compounded by the altitude.

Finally remember that much of Ladakh is a highly sensitive border area where India meets China and Pakistan. You are not allowed to go more than one mile north of the Srinagar-Kargil-Leh road. At Leh the road turns south through Upshi and eventually reaches Manali in Himachal Pradesh. You are not allowed more than one mile east of this Leh-Manali road. People who ignore these regulations, so the story goes, may find themselves in an unpleasant jail for a week or three before the authorities get around to telling them how naughty they've been.

PEOPLE
The Ladakhis are Tibetan-Mongoloid in appearance — a healthy looking people, deep brown in colouring due to the strong summer sun. Men traditionally wear a long woolen robe tied at the waist while women wear a similar robe but on their backs they add a colourful shawl — in which a baby or parcels can easily be carried. The women wear their hair in two long pigtails, a style also followed by some men. They top the picturesque ensemble with a top hat which somehow remains firmly balanced, perched on top of their heads. Although many men are abandoning their traditional dress for western clothing, the women still predominantly wear their colourful local dress. Many Ladakhis are nomads, herding their goats, noted for their fine Pashima wool, to high altitudes during the summer. Men carry the small essentials of Ladakhi life (flints, cap, tea cup, etc) either in their robe or hanging from their belt.

RELIGION
Although the Islamic influence extends out of the Kashmir Valley as far as Kargil in Ladakh, the predominant religion is overwhelmingly the Tibetan, Lamaist form of Buddhism. As the Kashmiris look towards Mecca, so do the Ladakhis look towards Lhasa and although it may be incorrect to refer to Ladakh as 'little Tibet' there is much evidence of Tibetan influence. This Lamaist influence extends to the use of Tibetan scrip for the holy books of Kandshur and the clear Tibetan architectural influence, particularly evident in the design of the Leh Palace which bears so many similarities to the larger Potala in Lhasa. Lamaism is a form of Buddhism heavily influenced by the pre-Buddhist Bon religion, of Tibet. This is especially noticeable on

a young and an old Ladakhi in Leh

the stones and banners which carry pictures and carvings of Bon demons and gods. At the pinnacle of the Lamaist pantheon is the divine trinity of Avalokitesvara, Manyushri and Vayrapani but there are an extraordinary number of other gods and demons. Their pictures totally cover the walls of many gompas and to further complicate matters there can be unique incarnations only recognised in certain gompas!

Lamaism is the monastic side of the religion, the study of which requires long hours of meditation by the monks. This essential basis of Lamaist Buddhism contrasts with the visible rituals which most Ladakhis observe, such as pilgrimages to gompas, chortens, mani-walls, and holy tombs, or turning prayer wheels and chanting mantras. The observance of their religion is an everyday occurrence in the life of the people of Ladakh.

Lamaism probably came to Ladakh around the 10th century. It has been the religion of Tibet since 632 AD under the reign of King Srong-btsan-sgam-po but had additions made to it under the influence of the magician Padmasambhava. Ladakhi monasteries belong to two main sects — the red-caps and the yellow-caps. The yellow-cap (or Gelugpa sect) are a reformed sect who follow the Dalai Lama as a reincarnation of the Boddhisattva Avalokitsevara.

In Leh it is possible to find families whose members are Moslems, Chris-

tians, and Buddhists since the Ladakhis are notably tolerant of other beliefs. As a rule, however where there are different religious groups in the
same area (as between Kargil and Shergol on the Srinagar-Leh road) they
live quite separately from one another and retain their own individuality.

GEOGRAPHY
The main settlements in Ladakh are strung along the Indus River Valley
which runs in an approximately north-west to south-east direction. In turn
the Zanskar range parallels the Indus Valley to the south and separates Ladakh from the Zanskar Valley. To the north-east of Ladakh is the high
Changtang plateau reached by a number of passes but this barren sparsely
populated area with its high altitude salt lakes is well into the restricted
zone of Ladakh. Much of it is under Chinese control. Only about 40 km
from Leh, but again deep into the restricted zone where foreigners may not
enter, is the lovely Nubra Valley noted for its apple, apricot and mulberry
trees. The valley is only accessible for a couple of months each year since it
is July before the snow melts back from the passes. Entry to the Nubra
Valley is either over the dangerous, due to the avalanches, Khardung La pass
at over 5300 metres or by the even higher (5500) Digar La Pass.

PHOTOGRAPHY
It is prohibited to take photographs of any military or strategic equipment
or installations. This includes military camps, soldiers, military vehicles,
bridges and even places or objects that in our eyes could be civilian installations — such as the radio broadcasting station in Leh. This prohibition is
strictly enforced and infringing it can result in the confiscation of cameras
and films.

In the gompas you can generally photograph whatever you please apart
from very holy places, such as the Gonkhang room of Matho Gompa, where
only monks are permitted to set foot. Nevertheless, you should exercise
great restraint during prayers since flashes of light and the clicks of camera
equipment are very disturbing.

THINGS TO BUY
You may dream of dance masks and tankas but you are not allowed to buy
them! Antique dolls, swords, monastic antiquities such as Buddha figures,
dance masks and tanksas are all banned from being purchased, dealt in or
taken out of Ladakh. Antiques are defined as being 100 or more years old.
New tanksas are now being produced but you must be able to prove that
they are new. There has been a terrible drain of the accumulated treasures
of the gompas due to the greedy actions of some over-wealthy and thoughtless tourists. The government has, belatedly, recognised the danger of
Ladakh losing much of its cultural heritage and departing visitors have their
baggage searched at Ladakh airport.

butter lamp vendor

There are many other items which you are free to purchase and export. Look for chang and tea-vessels, silver cups and butter churns, simply knitted carpets with Tibetan patterns or the mussel shells which serve as ornaments. For a few rupees you can buy a prayerflag or for a very large number of rupees you could invest in a new perag (they cost up to $10,000), the head-gear with hundreds of turquoise stones and silver pieces, worn at festivals and on special occasions. Or you may be satisfied with a tea kettle from the bazaar or search for silver-worked articles from China.

In practically all the gompas, during the tourist season, monks will have all sorts of items for sale — ranging from bells and locks to small drums and musical instruments. Since demand for 'authentic' items has outstripped supply you cannot be certain that anything is of any age. In any case 'authentic' items should be left where they belong — in Ladakh.

Prices in Ladakh are generally quite high. Although there is much Tibet-an and Ladakhi clothing, Tibetan jewellery and other Tibetan curios on sale you should familiarise youself with prices in Kashmir, Nepal, Dharamsala or other Tibetan centres before spending freely in Ladakh.

MONEY
Although there are banks with facilities for changing foreign currency in

Ladakh note that India's perennial shortage of change is particularly bad in Ladakh. Bring as many one and two rupee notes as possible with you. Free spending tourists have created the image that all foreigners have money to burn. This is hardly helped by the ridiculously high, by Indian standards, entry charges to all the Ladakhi gompas. Do not be too lavish with tips and donations. The inflation this brings about does not effect only tourists. Apart from in Leh changing foreign currency will be virtually impossible.

TIBETAN CALENDAR

Like ours the Tibetan calendar has 12 months but the months not only each have a different number of days but their length can vary from year to year! This makes comparisons between our calendar and their's rather difficult. Nevertheless, gompa festivals do fall at around the same dates each year — the important Hemis festival is usually in late June. Like the Chinese calendar the Tibetan years are named after animals in a cycle which repeats every twelve years. 1981 is the year of the sparrow — we'll then have the years of the dog, pig, rat, ox, tiger (or cat), rabbit, dragon, snake, horse, sheep and monkey before coming back to sparrow again.

Tibetan calendar in Tikse Gompa

FOOD

The staple food in Ladakh is *tsampa*, which is made by lightly roasting barley in a large metal pan, partly mixed with sand to prevent the barley catching alight. The barley is then sieved to remove the sand and the roasted grain is ground in a watermill. The resulting meal is sprinkled with *gurgur* (salt water) or mixed with a small amount of liquid to form cakes. *Chang* (a locally made beer) is often drunk with the tsampa. These dishes are called *cholak*.

If you eat in a local restaurant in Leh you will probably be offered the following dishes: *tsampa* — usually with salted butter tea, partially sweetened; *tukpa* — noodles with meat; *moe moe* — steamed dough, usually with meat in the middle; *pava* — salted pudding; *skir* — hotpot of meat, potatoes, grain and sometimes vegetables; *holkur* — Ladakhi biscuit made of sugar, nuts, grain meal and normally baked by the host himself to be served to the patrons. There is much Tibetan influence and you will find many Chinese-Tibetan dishes like chow mein or *kothay* — meat or vegetables wrapped in thin dough and fried or steamed.

You may be surprised to see potatoes served in Ladakh. They were brought in by Moravian Christian missionaries from Germany in the last century. There are still about 200 Christians in Ladakh today. Food can get a little boring in Ladakh, the variety of vegetables and fruit grown locally is very limited. Much food and produce comes up from Kashmir, but only in the summer when the passes are open, of course. Prices are naturally inflated. It's worth bringing in a few menu brighteners like bars of chocolate or cans of apple juice. Ladakh is as insanitary as anywhere else in India so take care where you eat and beware of fresh fruit and vegetables, drink water at your own risk! Even boiling water isn't such a positive method of purifying it at this altitude since the boiling point is much lower. Remember to keep your fluid intake up as you can easily become dehydrated.

Tea & Butter Tea

The tea habit initially came to Ladakh, as to all of Tibet, from Imperial China but due to the closing of the Tibetan border tea now comes from India. You may find Chinese/Tibetan tea smuggled over the border from Tibet on sale in the bazaar in Leh. It's more rare than expensive and the quality is not too high. The tea is often transported in pressed blocks which can frequently be seen as offerings in monasteries.

The traditional Ladakhi tea is made with butter and tastes more like a soup than our idea of tea. The tea is initially made very strong, brewed for a long time, then diluted to a drinkable strength. The tea is then put into a butterchurn, a wooden vessel about 15 cm in diameter and 80 cm long. A spoonful of salted butter is added and churned into the liquid. Every Ladakhi, no matter how poor, has his own tea vessel. In rich families the tea is served in three-part silver cups, the lower cup stands on a small pedestal and the cup itself is covered with a lid. The tea is generally drunk warm, not hot and during the colder part of the year the lower cup serves as a handwarmer.

If you are invited for tea anywhere in Ladakh you will find that your cup is refilled as soon as you take a sip. Tea is usually drunk during prayer ceremonies at gompas and you may be offered some, in that case you will be expected to have your own cup, an item every Ladakhi carries everywhere he or she goes.

making butter tea

Chang
Beware of the effects of the native beer — chang. High altitude and too
much alcohol do not mix well! Nevertheless you should try some of this
local alcoholic beverage. There is a chang 'pub' in Leh and the price is
around Rs 1 per bottle. You should also try chang in a village at some stage,
it usually tastes much better. In Ladakh you find, as in the other Himalayan
states (except Tibet) with a population which belongs to the Tibetan group,
no manufacture of spirit liquors. Chang is a beer, home-brewed from barley
and millet, partially seasoned by the addition of pepper and sugar. It is not
filtered before serving so dregs and grains are found 'swimming' in the
liquid. In short chang is a most unusual pleasure for the palate.

THE LADAKHI LANGUAGE
Ladakhi differs substantially from Tibetan although they belong to the same
family of language and Ladakhi is written in the Tibetan script. Dialects in
nearby villages are very distinct and preserve their individuality to this
day — a typical result of a society where few people travelled and there was
little exchange of information. In more widely separated towns, such as Leh
and Kargil, the speech is so different that the inhabitants of one can hardly
speak the dialect of the other.

There is one Ladakhi word you should learn even before you arrive since
you will use it many, many times each day. That is *jullay* — the all purpose
greeting that covers 'hello, goodbye, how are you,' and simply 'greetings.'
The Ladakhis are friendly, outgoing, spontaneous people and they call out
jullay to everyone they meet — local or foreigner.

Other words you may come across include *tugjascha* — thank you, *gompa* — monastery, *lama* — monk, *tschomoh* — nun, *tartscho* — flag, *geihling* —
flute, *thung* — horn, *spoz* — smoking sticks, *tarchan* — prayer flags. If you
shop in the market in Leh some words you may wish to use include *kanu* —
peas, *alu* — potatoes (Urdu or Hindi), *nungma* — large white radishes (a
staple Ladakhi vegetable), *labuk* — red radishes, *zong* — corn or wheat,
nass — barley, *pullgubbi* — cauliflower, *schann-ma* (or in Hindi *saratur-
man)* — carrot, *kuschutman* — kohlrabi. Finally *gella* is the word for good.

Om Mani Padme Hum
On thousands of prayer flags and mani stones in Ladakh you will see the
phrase 'Om Mani Padme Hum' written, carved or painted. You'll hear the
phrase murmured by the monks and believers in all monasteries. The generally accepted translation runs: 'Oh, thou jewel in the lotus.' It is usually
addressed to Buddha or to Avalokitsevara, his Tibetan incarnation. It is interesting to read the interpretation of this mantra by the clergyman Phunt-
sog, who went through training as a Buddhist lama before his conversion to
Christianity: Om — the syllable which represents the the basis of all being in
Indian thought, in Buddhist thought it represents the trinity of speech,
body and soul. Mani — the jewels which the god of the Tibetans holds in his
right hand. They are arranged as a garland of roses and symbolise the way to

holiness. Padme — the lotus flower which the god holds in his left hand. It is the symbol of purity. Hum — bless me. The whole phrase could thus be translated as 'Thou God with the jewel-rose-garland in one hand and the lotus flower in the other, bless my life, soul and spirit'!

GETTING THERE

Air Indian Airlines only started flying into Leh in 1979 — it's probably the highest airport in the world to be used regularly by jet airlines. The short, less than half an hour, flight is extremely spectacular as it goes right across the Himalayas with superb views of Nun and Kun almost directly below you and K2 (Mt Godwin Austin), the second highest mountain in the world, away to the north.

The flight costs Rs 286 but flying to Ladakh does have a few hassles. The weather in Leh is very changeable and unpredictable and the high winds that blow up virtually every afternoon means the flights can only be made in the mornings. Plus the approach is difficult, requiring clear visibility. Coming in you fly up the Indus Valley, the mountains rising above you on both sides, then turn left to the runway. Leaving Leh you have to bank right as soon as you're airborne because the Spitok monastery, perched on its hills, is just to the left of the runway end. Approaches and departures can only be made in one direction because the runway runs steeply uphill.

The end result is that flights to Leh are frequently cancelled or aborted after crossing the mountains. To compound the difficulties, Indian Airline's tight scheduling and insufficient number of aircraft means that it is difficult to put on extra flights if necessary or even to replace cancelled or aborted flights. At the start of the season in particular the twice weekly flights can be absurdly heavily booked — a full 737 load can be flown in but due to the altitude only a partial load can be taken out of Leh. Fortunately, at the beginning of the season the 'rush' is into Leh, not out. If you arrive in Srinagar planning to fly to Leh but without a reservation, or worse have a reservation but the flight is cancelled, you may have to do some heavy work to get on a flight. Baksheesh and money in the right hands is the name of the game in Srinigar — your houseboat/hotel owner or a local travel agent will know how to do it.

At the start of the '80 tourist season a typical week of flying to Leh went like this: Monday flight — aborted. Tuesday — extra flight put on but again aborted. Wednesday, Thursday, Friday — no extra flights but the unlucky Monday-Tuesday passengers had to keep reporting back to the IA office to find out what was happening. Saturday — regular flight goes OK but there was no room for any of the Monday-Tuesday passengers. Sunday extra flight but again it's aborted! Monday — regular flight gets through OK but with only a dozen or so of Monday-Tuesday's passengers. Tuesday — no extra flight. Wednesday — extra flight gets through and finally gets passengers, many of whom have been waiting in Srinagar for 10 days and have flown to Leh (unsuccessfully) on three occasions, to their destination. Some passengers had crossed the Himalayas seven times! Still a few years back it was not unknown for unlucky Ladakhis to make a last minute trip down to Srinagar in October only to get stuck there when the snow came unusually early. In that case you just had to sit and wait for six months before you could get home. Today they can fly back. The Indian Air Force flies to Leh from Chandigarh every day with a large transport aircraft — and their flight always gets in, bad weather or not.

Roads Buses depart from Srinagar for Leh every day during the season. Officially this is June to October but it's not unusual for the road to be closed until mid-June although on occasion it may be open by mid-May. The Zoji La pass is the last pass to be opened — although it is not the highest it is the one which gets the heaviest snow fall. The Namika La and Fatu La are within Ladakh, where precipitation is very light. There are A class (Rs 52) and B class (Rs 36) buses on the Srinagar-Leh route but there is little comfort difference between the two. A are four across seating with rudimentary headrests. B are five across seating. The trip takes two days with an overnight halt at Kargil where there are plenty of hotels. You leave at 7.30 am each morning and arrive at around 5 pm each evening. The total distance may be only 434 km but it's a winding, often steep, road. At high

Zoji La Pass

altitudes the buses often crawl uphill at a snail's pace.

You can easily hire jeeps to make the trip but they will cost something around Rs 1500 — they'll easily accommodate six passengers. If you take a jeep it's worth spreading the trip out by another day and making short forays off the main road to see some of the gompas along the way.

Before the Road Opens In the last few weeks before the Srinagar-Leh road opens it is possible to get to Ladakh by walking over the Zoji La Pass. The pass marks the boundary to dry Ladakh and is the last pass to be cleared of snow.

To get to the pass you can either hire a jeep from Srinagar (say Rs 500) or overnight in Sonamarg and in the morning get the 7 am Beacon Patrol Truck up to the pass. It's wise to try and latch on to a party of locals to ensure you follow the correct path. There will usually be somebody crossing every day and it's often possible to hire ponies or porters. Towards the end of the melt the walk may be only a couple of kms, taking a few hours, but early birds may have to walk for more than a day — sheltering at an army hut on the way. In 1980 a month before the road opened walking across entailed a 20 km trudge through the snow. In these early conditions the patrol may insist that you're adequately equipped and prepared before letting you cross.

You must take sunglasses and a good skin barrier cream. The deep snow and intense sunlight can easily lead to temporary snow-blindness or very bad sunburn. Late in the melt, or late on a hot day, you can get very wet from the slushy snow. Once over the pass you have to get a ride down to Drass. How easy this is depends on how many people are up at the pass working on the snow clearance. You'll quite possibly have to wait all day and if you're wet it will be an uncomfortable wait.

There's a tourist hut in Drass and next day you should be able to get a ride down to Kargil. From Kargil there are buses on to Leh but only on two days each week during the winter. The pass is actually cleared of snow for some time before the road is open to traffic however there are always road repairs to be done and debris, brought down with the snow, to be cleared. Jeeps can often cross the road before it is officially cleared for buses.

FROM SRINAGAR TO LEH

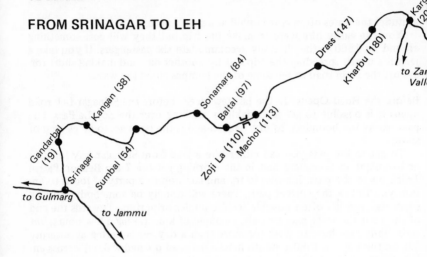

The road between the Kashmir Valley and Ladakh is surfaced almost all the way. It leaves Srinagar heading north-west and winds its way into the Sind Valley. The road goes through rice and maize fields and over partly submerged bridges — old wooden bridges over which the military have built Pioneer bridges — crossing the Sind River. It passes through the villages of Ganderbal, Kangan and Gund before reaching Sonamarg, the last sizeable settlement in the Kashmir Valley. The road was built after the 1962 Indo-Chinese conflict.

Sonamarg is less a place to stay than a jumping-off point for trekking tours and riding trips in the mountains; in winter it is a paradise for skiers. Popular trekking tours include Sonamarg-Armanath grotto, Sonamarg-Thajavas glacier, Sonamarg-Wangat. Beyond Sonamarg you reach the border to the Ladakh region.

The first pass, which the road approaches after many winding corners, is the Zoji-La (3529 metres). After rainfall or during the spring snow-melt, one must beware of rockslides on this 1000 metre ascent. Due to these rockfalls the road is very narrow in places and the Zoji-La Pass itself is not sealed. In 1978, due to bad weather, the stretch from Sonamarg to Kargil was in terrible condition. From the heights of the Zoji-La Pass, the road passes through the region where the Drass River has its source and along the river's valley. The first settlement after the pass is the town of Matayan on the Gumbar River, inhabited by Kashmiris, Dards and Baltis. The people speak Urdu, Dardi, Kashmiri and Balti. The further settlements are mostly on the mountain sides above the road, which passes through the villages of Prandrass and Murad Bagh before reaching Drass in a 15 square km valley.

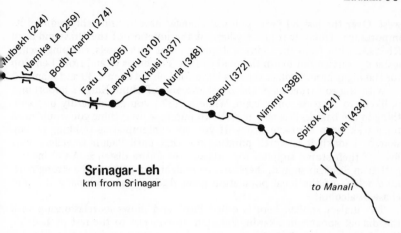

Srinagar-Leh
km from Srinagar

to Manali

Drass (147 km from Srinagar)
This is a small village with a TCP and a large military camp on the Drass River, en route to Kargil. The Public Works Department Rest House has a tourist officer and stands on the right hand side of the road from Srinigar. It can't be missed as it is directly opposite the Rahi Tea Stall where there is 'Hot Tea Available Anytime'. Drass is famed for its freezing temperatures and heavy winter snowfalls. In this area the dialect spoken is named after the weather — *Hambabs* means snowfall. For trekking from Drass to Sanku (Suru Valley) see the Zanskar section.

From Drass to Kargil the road follows the river. At a left-hand curve outside of Drass four 7th century Buddhist bas-reliefs stand next to the road: Maitreya, Avalokitesvera, an equestrian figure and a lotus. Beyond Tashgam the valley narrows and the mountain sides on both sides of the river are covered with rocks and pebbles. Shortly before the road from the Drass Valley turns off into the Suru Valley a reasonable bridge, passable by jeeps, crosses the Drass River towards the left. This bridge is barred to foreigners as it leads into a restricted military area.

From Drass the road runs to Kharbu (10 km), to Channigund (14 km) and then Kargil (10 km). The villages along the route are all hundreds of metres above the road, on small plateaux. Beyond Tashgam the landscape becomes more rocky, the mountains on both sides of the river reaching 5000 to 5500 metres.

Kargil (204 km from Srinagar, 2650 metres)
Kargil was once an important trading post due to its strategic location at the intersection of trade routes from Russia to India and from China to the

west. Over the last 30 years political changes have considerably reduced its importance. Today it is just a village at the junction of the Drass and Suru Rivers, 20 km from the Indus; a stopping point with hotels, camping facilities and a service station on the road to Leh. The buses to and from Leh stop for the night here. Civilian vehicles leave for Leh between 4.30 and 5 am.

With the construction of the Zanskar road to Padum, Kargil's importance is likely to increase once again. While in 1974 you could hardly buy anything in the bazaar, it is now possible to purchase everything you would need for a trek, even kerosene stoves. If you are contemplating trekking in Zanskar or Ladakh it is worth pointing out that until Padum travellers must live off their stored supplies for virtually the entire distance. Anything forgotten in Srinagar should, therefore, be bought here. Due to the strong religious beliefs of the local population great difficulties accompany the purchase of alcohol!

The dialect spoken here is called Purik and shows its relationship with the dialect spoken in Skardu, Pakistan. In contrast to the rest of Ladakh, the children here are taught in Arabic. A momentous occasion in Kargil is the archery contest in May. By the time one gets to Kargil the traveller will have been struck by the artificially irrigated fields. Since irrigation is so important in this region, the distribution of water requires great care. Every village is divided into groups, called Gowar, of from five to 10 families, to ensure an equitable arrangement. In Kargil itself the conspicuous absence of women in the streets is a consequence of Islamic religious practice. The people follow the Shi'ite Moslem sect, like the Iranians.

Kargil is the second largest town in Ladakh and has a population of about 3000. It's situated in a lovely valley with apricot trees growing in the intensively cultivated fields. Willows and poplars grow beside the irrigation ditches which lead to the terraced fields. They furnish building materials for the construction of houses in this nearly treeless land.

Trespone and Sankhoo are two 'Imanbaras' found in Kargil. These Turkish style buildings have Persian and Arabic speaking Moslem mystics known as Aghas in residence. Kargil also has a mosque, the Jami Masjid. Kargil's Moslems are noted for their extreme orthodoxy.

Accommodation

Kargil is a bit of a wild-west town and consists of just one main street so it's no problem finding anything. There are two popular cheaper hotels with prices from around Rs 15 for a double. The *Yak Tail* is rather dirty, the *Argalia* is better (cleaner!) value although it is uncomfortably close to Kargil's diesel electricity generator. Fortunately the power goes off at 11 pm.

Better hotels include the *Hotel D'Zojila*, which is 2.5 km from the town centre and has doubles from around Rs 75. The *Suru View*, behind the bus stand, is somewhat cheaper with doubles from Rs 40. There's also a *Dak Bungalow*, reserved mainly for official use, and several other hotels. Kargil has two banks, there are no banking facilities in Soñamarg or anywhere between Kargil and Leh.

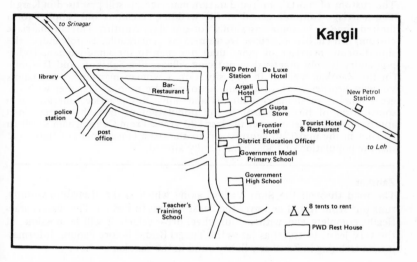

Other Accommodation along the Srinagar-Leh Road
Drass has a Rest House with three double rooms as does Bodh Kharbu, neither have running water. At Mulbekh there is a four room Rest House. Saspul has a small restaurant. At Sanku on the Kargil-Zanskar route there is a two room Rest House.

Around Kargil
Mount Kala Pahad (4575 metres) near to Kargil, was under Pakistani control until the 1971 India-Pakistan conflict. In that war the borders of India were pushed further to the west but one still cannot travel directly to the Indus valley and along the Indus to Leh. One must still take the hard way over the Namika-La and Fatu-La passes and reach the Indus valley by Khalsi. At present a road is being built around the Namika-La pass — 'which touches the sky'. It runs through the forbidden zone, west of the present road. In this region are the interesting villages of Garkon, Dards, Dardchik and Dha Hanoo, whose population (altogether about 700 people) is light skinned and speaks a language which sounds like Russian although it also contains elements of Persian and Sanskrit, the languages of the Aryan invaders. The remote locality and the custom of marrying only amongst themselves has preserved their distinctive identity right up to the present day. The government of the village is the responsibility of a seven-man village council, chosen by all men in the village. In July these villages celebrate a harvest festival which lasts for several days. Garkon is 80 km from Kargil.

Muta & Polyandry

The custom of 'muta', limited-duration marriages, is still practised in Kargil. The marriage contract signed at the wedding ceremony only applies for a limited time — in some cases only for one day. Another Tibetan marriage custom, which often strikes westerners as remarkable, is polyandry, the simultaneous marriage of more than one man to the same woman. Today polyandry is only practised in outlying villages like Saliskote and Trespone (in the Zanskar region). In this situation a woman marries her husband's younger brothers, except for any who may be monks. Together with the great number of unmarried monks and nuns, this practice functions as a social form of birth control — the population of Ladakh has remained approximately constant over the last 120 years. From Cunningham's visit to Ladakh in the mid-19th century, up to the latest Government of India census, the population of Ladakh has hardly altered.

Zanskar

The road through the Suru Valley, along which is the Rangdum Gompa, runs out from Kargil and over the Pensi-La pass to Padum. The road is practically complete and with a four-wheel drive vehicle it will be possible, at the very least, to travel as far as the Tungri Bridge before Padum. Information on trekking in Zanskar will be found in the Zanskar section.

Kargil-Shergol

The road starts to climb shortly after Kargil and leaves the Suru Valley over a small pass in the Wakkha Valley. Here you cross the religious border and see the first Ladakhis with their typical Tibetan-headgear.

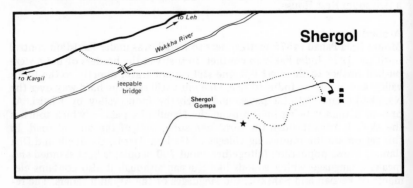

A   Hazratbal Mosque by Dal Lake
B   Houseboats on Dal Lake

Shergol (237 km from Srinagar)

The small village of Shergol is 33 km from Kargil. The village, on the right hand side of the Wakkha River, is hard to see from the road as it lies behind a mountain. A small gompa perches half-way up the eastern slope of this mountain — appropriate to its size the gompa has only two monks who are tended by a single nun. Some of the rooms, such as the kitchen, are hewn from the rock and resemble holes more than rooms. The gompa has some beautiful wall paintings which are well worth seeing. At the foot of the mountain, near the 35-house village (210 inhabitants), there is a less important gompa.

Mulbekh (244 from Srinagar)

A further seven km brings you to this Wakkha Valley village. The palace of Rajah Chalon of Mulbekh is on the left hand side of the road. Above the village on the slopes is a double monastery. It's a difficult ascent, particularly if you are not yet acclimatised to the altitude of Ladakh. Two paths

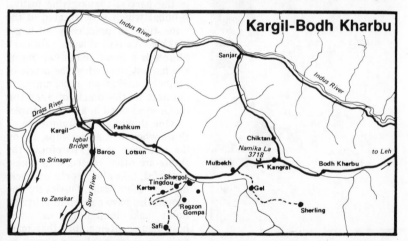

lead to the gompa and the right hand path (monastery mountain to the left) is the easier. Here, as with all gompas in Ladakh, one should make enquiries beforehand in the village as to whether the monks are present. Often the gompas may be deserted for days at a time and therefore shut. Only in the mornings and evenings can one be sure of encountering lamas who are not

A Main street in the hill resort of Pahalgam
B The Lidder River between Pahalgam and Aru
C Jami Masjid Mosque in Srinagar

Chamba statue at Mulbekh

engaged in prayer. We were able to put two lamas of Mulbekh Gompa into action by showing them pictures of the Dalai Lama. These pictures of a holy person are, naturally, also holy and are handled accordingly — carefully touched, pressed on the forehead and reverentially returned. With amazing speed the lamas then ascended the mountain and opened the gompas (the Serdung and Gandentse Gompas) for us.

Choose the direct path up to the gompas even though it seems steep for it gives a better view of the Wakkha Valley. A festive highpoint is the harvest thanksgiving festival (Shuba) which is celebrated at the same time in practically all larger Wakkha Valley villages. Mulbekh Shubla is a great attraction during the harvest time when the oracle of Mulbekh makes an appearance. In contrast to the oracle of Shey this one is incarnated in a young farmer.

One should always remove one's shoes when visiting a gompa. If you do not like going barefoot, the floors are often coated with rancid butterfat, take along socks or stockings for these visits. Obviously one should also have a reverent attitude; don't make loud noises or touch holy figures. Remember that mani walls or chortens should always be walked around clockwise with the structure on your right.

Chamba Statue
A km beyond Mulbekh, beside the road on the right hand side, is a huge figure of the Matriya, or future, Buddha, cut into the rock. The figure is thought to date from Kushan period, around the time of the birth of Christ. Inscriptions found on the side of the rock are in the Kharoshti script. A new small temple, which partly obscures the figure was built in 1975.

Gel

If you wish to make more than a short pause at Mulbekh and to experience a little of the local way of life then visit the village of Gel. The small village, picturesquely situated on a steep slope above the Wakkha River, still lives (like many Ladakhi villages) in a bygone era. Although it is only a few km from the surfaced road Indian soldiers rarely come here and during a visit there time seems to stand still. When we visited Gel not only did the children cry when they first saw us, but adults held the animals fast in their quarters, barricaded the doors and observed us suspiciously from the roofs of their houses. The ice was rapidly broken, however, when we wanted to buy an expensive Giri (hand-spindle with distaff). With the construction of the new jeep-road to the Namika-La, the modern world is now encroaching upon Gel.

Mulbekh-Lamayuru via the Namika La & Fatu La

From Mulbekh the road climbs through a sandhill landscape to the 3718 metre high Namika La. The first village beyond the pass is Kangral; a small collection of houses where it may be possible to obtain fuel. Here also a dirt road branches to the left, leading to Stakchey, Samra, Chiktan (with old palace ruins), Sihakar, Sanjar and along the Indus to eventually meet the Kargil-Khalsi road. The principal town in the valley of the Kanji

Lamayuru Gompa

Nallah is Bodh Kharbu, a large military camp which stretches out on both the right and left sides of the road. In the resthouse of the PWD, on the left hand side of the road, the two travellers' rooms can sometimes be used by tourists. There are many government projects underway during the beautiful summer months so your chances of finding a room free are not good.

The road follows the river for a short time and then winds its way to the 4094 metre high Fatu La pass, which is always cool and windy. This is the highest pass on the Srinagar-Leh road. About 15 km from the top of the pass the old Tibetan monastery of Lamayuru stands below the road on a crumbling mountain. There is a village on the mountain side.

Lamayuru (310 km from Srinagar, admission Rs 5)

According to an old legend there was, in the valley of Lamayuru, in the time of the Sakyamuni Buddha, a crystal clear lake where the nagas lived. Arahat Madhyantaka prophesied that in later times a monastery would be built there and through a supernatural force he emptied the lake. In the 10th century Naropa, one of the 80 wise men, visited the Valley of Lamayuru and spent many years meditating in a hut.

The first Lamayuru monastery was built under Rinchen Zangbo at the end of the 10th century, under orders from the king of Ladakh who altogether had 108 gompas built in West Tibet. It was built on the broken mountain in the valley and consisted of five buildings, of

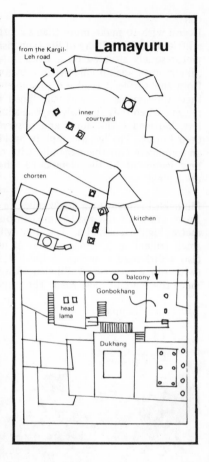

Lamayuru Gompa

which only the central building stands today. One can still see some remains of the four corner buildings to the west. The gompa has an impressive 11 headed, 1000 eyed image of Chanrazik. In its heyday up to 400 monks lived in the monastery but today there are only 20 to 30 who belong to the yellow sect. Many lamas from Lamayuru now go out to other parts of Ladakh as teachers.

In the 16th century the monastery was declared a holy site in which even criminals could seek sanctuary. For that reason even today it is known to Ladakhis as Tharpa Ling, 'Place of Freedom'. Although the monastery has some fields they are insufficient to feed all the monks. Therefore, like practically all other Ladakhi monasteries, they are dependent upon the donations of believers. In order to channel these donations small daughter gompas were erected in outlying villages, their superior lama being the head lama at Lamayuru. Similarly the Sankar Gompa in Leh is an 'under-gompa' of the Spitok Gompa. Several time each year the monks from all the under-gompas come to Lamayuru for general prayers. These colourful occasions, when mask dancing goes on for three days, fall in the second month of the Tibetan calendar (March) and in the fifth month (July).

The Drogpo Valley and Lamayuru Gompa first come into sight 14 km beyond the Fatu La pass. The road leads into the village of Lamayuru and on into the valley a short distance beyond this viewpoint. If you do not have a four-wheel drive vehicle and wish to go to the monastery you must continue a few km further along the main road towards Leh. A steep route then leads to the right into the valley, again for four-wheel drive only. It ends at a low, small gateway into a small inner courtyard. Before this gate there is nowhere for a vehicle to turn around. If you wish to see more than just the gompa you should descend to the valley where the village (population about 500) follows its medieval lifestyle at the foot of the monastery mountain.

You should also take a short walk into the fields to see the mani walls, being sure to pass the wall on the left side — ie with the wall on your right. Here at Lamayuru it is interesting that the mani walls, piled up by devout pilgrims, stone by stone, often dragged there from many km away, and with the mantra 'Om mani padme hum' carved on them, have more than a religious significance. These stone walls protect the fields in the valley bottom from the avalanches which can be loosened by snow and rain. Similar mani-guard-walls can be seen past Khalsi and at Hemis. Leh has the longest mani-walls but it is no longer possible to walk the full pilgrim path of several km because it leads into military areas.

Khalsi (Khalatse, 337 km from Srinagar)
Beyond Lamayuru, the military road winds round many sharp curves, the so-called Langro Curves, on a slope in a side valley of the Indus, then crosses over a barren rocky slope to the river banks. Beware the speedbreakers before the last curve! Near the ruins of old fortifications, with the remains of a

hanging bridge, the road crosses a stable iron bridge on the right bank of the Indus. After some sharp bends it passes through a military camp close to where the Khalsi-Gurgurod road branches off to the left. This road will eventually lead directly to Kargil, avoiding the Fatu La and Namika La passes, Khalsi today is a rest stop for buses and has many restaurants on the main road offering reasonably priced food — usually dal and rice.

Rizong

The Rizong monastery is 32 km from Khalsi. One travels 26 km further on towards Leh to the settlement of Ulay Tokpo where there are four houses and a camp set up by Sita World Travels. Two hundred metres before this spot a route branches off into a northern side-valley of the Indus. On foot the route crosses the river after 10 minutes. On the right side, after a further 50 minutes, you reach Julichen, a nunnery in an apricot grove. By car you can travel from the highway to within two km of here before being halted by a bridgeless crossing — a bridge is due to be completed very soon.

The nunnery belongs to the Rizong Gompa and inside the courtyard you will find nuns busy spinning wool. At the fork in the road beyond Julichen, marked by a blue flagpole and several coloured mani-stones, turn to the left. On both sides of the road you will see painted inscriptions on the rock face.

mandala in Rizong Gompa

A further 30 minutes climb in a barren side valley will bring you to the first Rizong chorten. A sign in English instructs you to 'Refrain from smoking, drinking and eating here'. The small valley then opens into a depression on whose southern slope stands the monastery.

Founded in 1829 the monastery is at 3450 metres and presently has 30 monks. Its head lama belongs to the Shas Rimpoche in Dharamsala and the Chuldchim Nima in Manali. After the Thekchen workshop room the Duk-hang is the most important room in the monastery. One reaches it up some steps which end on a balcony-type vestibule. On another level one can see the stone drum with which the Rizong monks beat out their prayers. The stone drum is made of a hollowed out tree stump which has been covered with a stone slab. It is hit with a small stone hammer.

Women are not allowed to stay overnight at the Rizong Gompa. They must take quarters in the Julichen nunnery.

Alchi
A road leads off the highway to a bridge over the Indus at a point 33 km beyond Khalsi and two km before Saspul. The old bridge, which can only be crossed in a small jeep, is to be replaced by a new bridge which buses will be able to use. Travellers will then be able to travel directly to Alchi along the new graded road. In the village of Alchi there are many chortens, some of which possess gatelike openings and others have the bases of small towers at their four corners. Alchi is unusual in that it is on lowland, not perched on a hill top like other Ladakhi gompas. Built in the 11th century it is noted for its massive statues of Buddha and its lavish wood carvings and art-work — almost baroque in style.

Saspul (372 km from Srinagar)
Cave dwellings and a small fort can be seen on the left side of the road.

Lekir
The Lekir Gompa turn off is 9.5 km from Saspul. The steep road has many hairpin bends and normal vehicles can only cover the first 2.5 km after which four-wheel drive is required for the remaining stretch beyond the small river bridge. The bridge over the Lekir River is not very stable. There are approximately 100 yellow-cap lamas belonging to the gompa. At Lekir the monks ring out their prayers by hitting a wooden beam which they use as a bell.

The gompa school has 30 pupils who learn three other languages beside Ladakhi. They are Tibetan for religious purposes, Hindi and English. The pupils, who are prepared as recruits for the monastery, live part of the time with their parents and part of the time in the monastery. The Indian government also has two elementary schools in Lekir village. There are three grades of lamas — Chunjung, then Gyetsul and the highest grade — Gyelong.

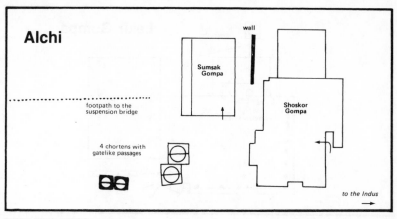

Alchi

wall

Sumsak Gompa

Shoskor Gompa

footpath to the suspension bridge

4 chortens with gatelike passages

to the Indus

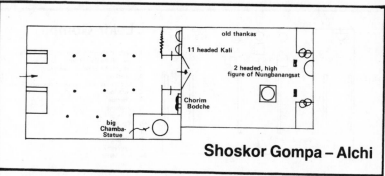

old thankas

11 headed Kali

2 headed, high figure of Nungbanangsat

Chorim Bodche

big Chamba-Statue

Shoskor Gompa – Alchi

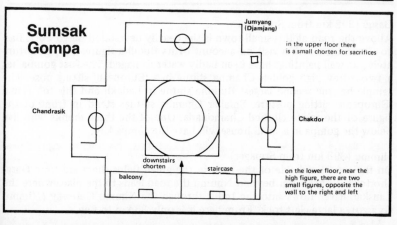

Sumsak Gompa

Jumyang (Djamjang)

in the upper floor there is a small chorten for sacrifices

Chandrasik

Chakdor

downstairs chorten

staircase

balcony

on the lower floor, near the high figure, there are two small figures, opposite the wall to the right and left

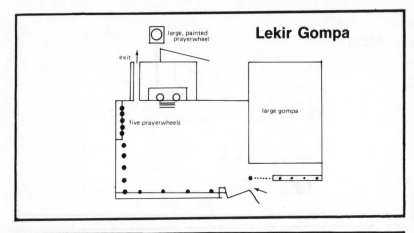

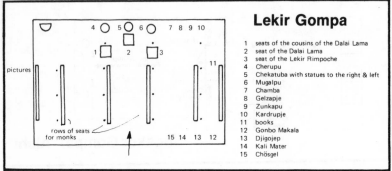

Lekir Gompa

1. seats of the cousins of the Dalai Lama
2. seat of the Dalai Lama
3. seat of the Lekir Rimpoche
4. Cherupu
5. Chekatuba with statues to the right & left
6. Mugalpu
7. Chamba
8. Gelzapje
9. Zunkapu
10. Kardrupje
11. books
12. Gonbo Makala
13. Djigojep
14. Kali Mater
15. Chösgel

Basgo (392 km from Srinagar)

Above the road at this small town is the heavily devastated Basgo Fort. Basgo Gompa is worth a visit on account of its Buddha figures but, unfortunately, its wall paintings have been badly water damaged. The first gompa has a two-storey high golden Chamba statue in a 'European' sitting pose. The temple has the second largest Buddha statue in Ladakh and this too is in a 'European' sitting posture. Smaller Chamba statues stand in front of the figure of the white clothed Chamonada. One of the three monks who live below the gompa in a small house will have the gompa key.

Nimmu (398 km from Srinagar)

On the right hand side of the road in the green fields there are four 'Gate' chortens. Just 2.5 km beyond Nimmu the road leads to the place where the Zanskar River flows into the Indus through the Nimmu Gateway (Nimmu Gyasgo), a large cleft rock. From here it is only 35 km to Leh.

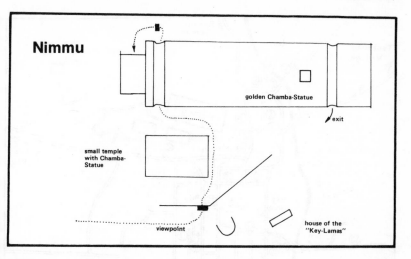

Nimmu

golden Chamba-Statue

exit

small temple
with Chamba-
Statue

viewpoint

house of the
"Key-Lamas"

LEH

The capital of Ladakh, Leh is about 10 km north-east of the Indus at the exit of a fertile side-valley. From the town down to the Indus, the landscape is almost completely barren. Leh (3505 metres) has a population of 8500 and a large military camp stands between the town and the airfield, which is also down towards the Indus. There are a number of interesting places to visit in and around this fascinating town but it is equally interesting just to wander the winding back streets of the old town. At one time Leh was a major stopping point on the Asian 'silk route' and a commercial capital in its own right. Today it's important mainly for its military base but also, more recently, as a tourist centre.

Leh Palace

The old palace of the kings of Ladakh (open 6-9 am and from 5 pm) over-looks the town from the south-west slope of the Tsenmo hill. It has eight storeys and was built by King Singe Namgyal in the 16th century, at much the same time as the famed Potala of Lhasa — which it resembles. The dam-age to the palace, one side is gaping open, stems from the Kashmiri invasions of the last century. Like the Shey Palace the Leh palace still belongs to the Ladakhi royal family, who now live in their palace in Stok.

Few of the palace wall paintings are worth looking at since they have been scratched and smeared over the years. The small Khar Gompa within the palace is also of little interest. In fact the main reason to make the short, steep climb up to the palace is for the superb views from the roof, over which the coloured prayer flags wave in the wind, the lines of which begin on the blue-white-red-green-yellow Tarchock mast. Beware of the many holes in the floors while you're wandering around the palace. In good

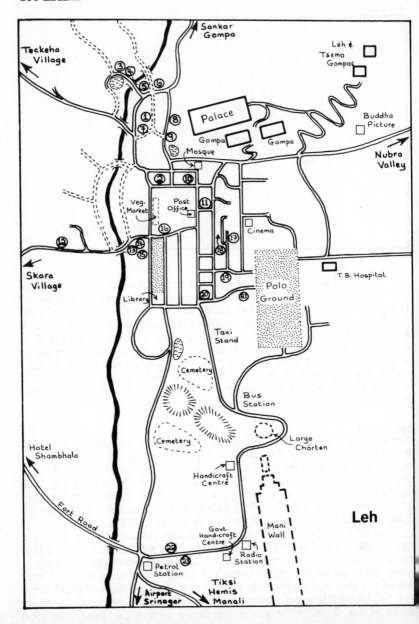

Leh

weather the Zanskar range, snow covered until early summer, appears close enough to touch although it rises from the other side of the Indus.

Leh Town

The old town of Leh, with its houses for the aristocrats and servants of the royal household, is clustered at the bottom of the hill under the palace. The new city spreads away from the hill on land which once belonged to the royal family. Due to steady growth in recent years, Leh is becoming increasingly westernised. At one time Leh had a city wall with three gates one of which still stands close to the market — to the right and uphill towards the palace. The gate is called Kingsgate because only the king and his family were allowed to use it. The chorten above the city is the remains of a royal leisure site.

Leh Gompa

High above the palace and also overlooking the ruins of the older palace of the king of Tagpebums. The Red Gompa (Tsemo Gompa) was built in 1430 by King Gvags-Pa-Bum-Ide and has a fine three-storey high seated Buddha figure flanked by Avalokitsevara on the right and Manjusri on the left. The walls have recently been brightly painted and the gompa is open from 7 am to 9 am and 5 to 7 pm. The gompa above it is in a very ruined condition but offers extremely fine views over Leh and the surrounding countryside. To the right of the palace you can see a Buddha painted on the rocks, a remnant of an earlier monastery.

Other Leh Gompas

There are a number of lesser gompas in the old town of Leh — such as the Guru Lakhang to the left of the palace, beneath the large chorten. The Chamba Lakhang, south of the palace, and the Chenrezig Lakhang, to the south-east, are similarly neglected since they contain little of interest compared to other more splendid gompas around Leh.

1	Police	13	Palace View Guest House
2	State Bank	14	Dreamland Hotel & Restaurant
3	Hotel Glacier View	15	Hotel Khangir & Restaurant
4	Hotel Karakoram	16	Indian Airlines
5	Hotel Shangrila	17	Apsara Guest House
6	Himalayan Hotel	18	Moonland Guest House
7	Khan Lodge	19	New Gay Time Restaurant
8	Hotel Khar Dungla	20	Barmar Restaurant
9	Ali Shah's Postcards	21	Palace View (Kidar) Hotel
10	Hilltop & Mumtaz Restaurants	22	Tibet Hotel
11	Antelope Guest House	23	Leh Motel
12	Hotel La Ri Mo		

Leh Fort
The Leh fort, built by Zorawar Singh, contains three temples but cannot be visited because it is within the military camp area.

Funeral Ceremonies
Near to the palaces at Stok, Shey and Leh you may notice a large number of chortens, the old 'pleasure gardens' of the kings of Ladakh. If you go into the side valley, to the north-east of Leh, on whose eastern slopes the road to the Nubra Valley begins, you may find (particularly with the help of a local) a large stone where a curious funeral practice was once conducted. The bodies of the dead were hacked to pieces and ground up with stones then left to be devoured by vultures. This practice was also followed in Tibet and is still followed in the Mustang region of Nepal. Today the site of dismemberment is used for cremations. After a ceremony in the house of the dead person the corpse is tied up in a covered sedan chair. Accompanied by lamas the procession makes its way into the side valley near Leh. A few hundred metres north-west of the chortens the procession halts and the chair is placed in a walled oven. This is really only a vertical tube with a firehole underneath. The fire is started with many prayers and during the long ceremony oil is frequently thrown into the oven until the cremation is complete. The ashes are scattered into a holy river or, in the case of a person of high standing, placed in a chorten.

Accommodation in Leh
There are quite an amazing number of hotels and guest houses in Leh and it is also relatively easy to arrange accommodation in private homes. Indeed many of the smaller guest houses are simply private homes which rent the odd room out. Prices are extremely variable, dropping right down in the off-season when there are very few visitors in Leh and shooting up in the high-season. Many places close down completely over the winter. Prices quoted below are for the high-season, cheaper places may halve (or more) their rates during the off-season although the more expensive hotels are less likely to be so variable.

As Leh's status as an international attraction grows the number of 'upper notch' hotels is rapidly increasing. Most of Leh's more expensive hotels are very new, almost without exception they quote all-inclusive prices with all meals. There is not a great choice of restaurants in Leh. The *Shambala Hotel* was taken over by the Oberoi chain in 1980 and has been considerably upgraded. Nightly costs are Rs 295/395 for singles/doubles including all meals. The Shambala is rather a long way out of town, off towards the edge of the valley.

Two recently completed hotels closer to the centre are the *Kang-Lha-Chhen* (tel 39) where singles/doubles are Rs 255/310 and the *Hotel Lha-Ri-Mo* where the cost is Rs 240/290. They're both within easy walking distance of the centre of Leh. The fourth more expensive hotel is the *Hotel Indus*, out of town on the Hemis road.

In the middle price category there is the *Khangri Hotel*, just down the road from the tourist office and uncomfortably close to the diesel generator. As in Kargil the power goes off around 11 pm. Doubles are in the Rs 70 to 100 bracket, room only. The side-by-side *Glacier View* and *Karakorum* are similarly priced. They're fairly close to the centre and both have pleasant gardens, an attraction shared by many of Leh's hotels. The *Hotel Yak Tail* is also in this price category and is next to the Dreamland Hotel, on the road leading to the Lha-Ri-Mo.

With rooms in the Rs 40 to 50 bracket (none of them with attached baths), a pleasant garden and the best restaurant in town, the *Dreamland* is a very popular hotel choice and also very close to the centre.

In the rock bottom category you can find doubles under Rs 30 (under Rs 20 in the off-season) and dormitory beds at Rs 5. Some places in this bracket also provide bed bugs at no extra cost so take care! Popular cheapies include the *Palace View Kidar Hotel*, close to the polo ground. It also has a collection of braying donkeys for your night time entertainment but it's 'run by a lovely woman who usually meets the bus dressed in her traditional costume. You eat meals in her elaborate kitchen, lovely breakfasts; nice atmosphere.' There's a second, unrelated, Palace View Hotel on the other side of the polo ground. The *Antelope Guest House* is on the main street of Leh, a stone's throw from the mosque, and has dorm beds for Rs 5. The *Moonland Guest House* is in the upper-cheap bracket, the *Old Ladakh Guest House* (quite close by) is similarly priced — both in the old part of town.

There are many, many other hotels all around the town — some in the winding, narrow streets of the old town; others out in the rice paddies to the other side of town. Leh also has several 'official' places which you are less likely to get in to: there's a *Dak Bungalow*, in which the tourist office is located, and the *Leh Motel* out towards the airport.

Wedding Ceremonies

A visitor to Ladakh rarely has a chance to see a Buddhist wedding performed according to the old customs and ceremonies. Today too much foreign influence is likely to have crept in, European clothing is slowing replacing the traditional dress. In 1975 we were fortunate enough to be guests at a wedding performed according to the old rites.

The celebration began at 10 pm in the house of the bride. The all male party celebrated with chang which, according to custom, one must take in three consecutive draughts. As a special sign the host improved the chang by adding butter. A celebration meal was served at 2 am but again only men partook. The bride remained in her mother's kitchen, symbolically indicating where her place was! Clothed in a wedding gown with a silver-embroidered cape, decorated with old family jewellery, the bride is overwhelmed with lucky white ribbons (kataks) and given gifts of money by her relatives and friends. While the men sing and the mother laments, the bride then goes to the family of the bridegroom, where she is met, in front of the house, by lamas.

Now the proper celebration begins. In a long ceremony, in which the bride must first of all refuse the food which is offered to her, the bride is led from her father or a friend of the family, to her husband, with whom she then symbolically partakes of a meal. She is then shown the house, with particular emphasis on the (her) kitchen. By sunrise the ceremony is concluded, but not the celebration which is a social occasion for the families with musicians, food and much, much chang.

Places to Eat in Leh

Leh is not going to win any eating out prizes, the choice is not wide nor the standards high. Far and away the best place to eat is the *Dreamland Restaurant*, right by the *Dreamland Hotel* and only a few steps from the Indian Airlines office. It's clean, friendly and very reasonably priced — most dishes are Rs 5 to 10. Tibetan kothay, various chow meins and other noodle dishes top the bill and make a pleasant change from rice, rice and more rice. They also do nice jasmine tea.

Almost next door to it is the *Khangri Restaurant* which is nice (but not quite so nice) and fairly cheap (but not quite so cheap). Good for a change of pace. After that the standards drop rapidly. The *Hilltop* right at the mosque and palace end of the street, is merely so-so — a popular coffee and chat place for locals but little else. The *Mumtaz* Restaurant, down below it gets good reports. There are many little places around the town centre and a string of Indian restaurants at the bottom end of the main street selling good Indian sweets and remarkably insanitary looking food. OK for a cup of tea but take care with anything else.

The *New Gaytime* (great name) is new and reasonably good, it's upstairs. Good tea, not so good snacks at the *Mini Cafe* by Indian Airlines.

Or you can buy fresh vegetables from the pavement across from the Hilltop Restaurant. There's a more official vegetable market too. Early in the morning you can get delicious hot, freshly baked bread from the cluster of little bakery stalls in the back streets by the mosque. It's cooked Middle East style in hole-in-the-ground ovens and is great for breakfast with honey — bring the latter with you from Srinagar.

Schools

Besides the monastery schools the Indian government has 380 educational establishments including over 200 primary schools in Ladakh. In 1971 literacy in Ladakh was still only 14%. There are over 200 Ladakhi students at universities in Srinagar, Jammu and elsewhere in India. They receive a

monk school in Lekir Gompa

monthly stipend of Rs 75 from the Indian government. We always found it interesting to visit the primary schools. We took some film in the village school at Parka, I photographed a schoolgirl standing with the typical wooden panel on which they write with a wooden stylus and thinned clay-liquid. The pupils draw a line for writing in a noteworthy manner — a string with chalk rubbed in is pressed onto the board and then plucked like a musical string. The result is a very sharp line. The Tibetan alphabet is learned by the pupils singing together.

GETTING AROUND

There is a reasonably extensive bus service around Ladakh although the J&K transport service seems to supply Ladakh with its oldest and most unreliable buses so breakdowns are not uncommon. There are also many jeeps, and a few taxis operating out of Ladakh. Count on Rs 3 or 4 per km for a jeep, or hire one by the day for Rs 250 or 300. In a day you can easily visit the Shey, Tikse, Hemis and Spitok Gompas by jeep and split between six people the cost is not so excessive. There is a bus service out to the airport for Rs 2 or a jeep would cost Rs 25.

Some bus costs from Leh include: *Kargil* — Rs 20 to 22, daily in summer, Sunday and Thursday in winter. *Choglamsar & Bridge* — 70p, fairly frequently each day. *Hemis* — Rs 6.50, departs 10 or 11 am from Leh, the bus goes to Sakti but you have to hop off at Karu and cross the Karu bridge, and walk six km up to the gompa. The bus returns from Sakti at 2 or 2.30 pm in the afternoon so you can't get to Hemis and back by bus on the same day. *Spitok* — 70p, twice daily. *Shey* — Rs 1.15, three times daily. The bus continues on to *Tikse* (Rs 1.50 from Leh) which is only a couple of km further out, you could easily bus to Shey, walk on to Tikse then bus back to Leh — or vice verse. Note that Shey Gompa is only open (officially) from 7 to 9 am. *Stok* — twice daily. *Phyang* (Fiang) — Rs 2.75, daily. *Khalsi* — Rs 7, alternate days. *Matho* — Rs 2.55, daily. *Chochot* (other bank of the Indus, between Stok and Stakna) — Rs 2 daily.

AROUND LEH

Sankar Gompa (3 km, entrance fee Rs 5)

This small but interesting Leh gompa can easily be visited on foot. The Sankar Gompa is an under-gompa of Spitok Gompa. At the most only 20 monks live here and few are permanently in residence. Thus the gompa is only open to the public (except on holidays) from 6 am to 8 am and from 6 to 7 pm. It is, however, well lit so an evening visit is worthwhile. From the yard you climb the steps to the front room or Dukhang. Double doors lead into the Dukhang proper. Three green drums immediately attract the eye, under which, to the right of the door, is the place of the Gyeskos. From the seat of the head lama, who is also the head lama of the Spitok Gompa, there is a good view of the richly painted wall and entrance door.

The upper floor of the gompa has the Dukar Lakhang with a Dukar figure — a most impressive representation of Avalokitesvara (also known as Chanrazik) complete with 1000 arms (all holding weapons), and 1000 heads. The walls of the room are painted with mandalas, a Tibetan calendar and rules for the monks. Above a wooden stairway you can also see the residence rooms of the head lama next to the guest rooms and the library.

Spitok Gompa (10 km from Leh, entrance fee Rs 10)

There are 125 yellow-cap monks at this monastery which stands on a small

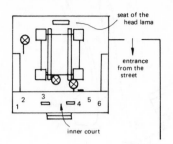

Sankar Gompa

seat of the head lama

entrance from the street

inner court

Demon wallpaints at the entrance to the Sankar Gompa Dukhang:

1 Stpekhorio
2 Namthosas
3 Memikzang
4 Fakskeypo
5 Yulkhor Rsung
6 Tsering Tokskor

⊗ three green ceremonial prayer wheels — next to these you find a prayer mast and a lama often sits by the door to guard the artwork.

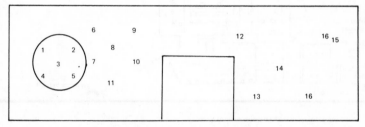

From the middle of the Dukhang to the wall with the entrance you see:

1-5 Gyapo Skuna
6 Gonkar
7 Lchamsing
8 Gonbo
9 Namsas
10 Zalzi

11 Khor
12 Chosgyal
13 Nezer
14 Jikjet
15 Paldanlamo
16 Chusen Singdongma

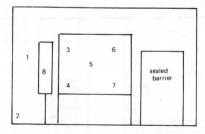

sealed barrier

Back room

1 Zongapa
2 Buddha
3 Gyatsap
4 Cho Rinpoche
5 Tsonkapa
6 Khatupze
7 Cho Rinpoche
8 Padmasambhava

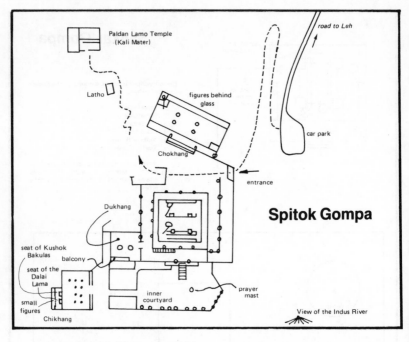

Spitok Gompa

Wallpaintings in the high prayer room of Spitok Gompa:

1 Maharkala
2 Jame Daka
3 Maharkala
4 Jamaransa
5 Setapa
6 Kali Devi
7 Chamching
8 Wamchass

1 2 3 4 5 6 7 8

entrance

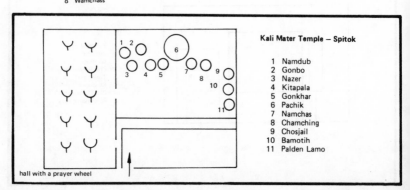

Kali Mater Temple – Spitok

1 Namdub
2 Gonbo
3 Nazer
4 Kitapala
5 Gonkhar
6 Pachik
7 Namchas
8 Chamching
9 Chosjail
10 Bamotih
11 Palden Lamo

hall with a prayer wheel

mountain above the Indus. You pass it on the way into Leh on the right hand side of the road and it's also very close to the end of the Leh airport runway. You can walk to the monastery from Leh in two hours but take care not to wander into the military zones.

There is the grave of a very high reincarnation at the gompa and the Spitok head lama is also the head lama of the Sankar Gompa in Leh. He also represents Ladakh as a member of the Indian Parliament. Spitok Gompa has three chapels of which the highest, the Paldan Lamo Temple (Kali Mater), is the most impressive. The temple (Gonkhang) is approximately a thousand years old. From the highest point on the Spitok hill you have a good view over the Indus Valley, the village of Spitok at the foot of the hill, of Pharka lying opposite, of the mountains, usually snow-covered even in summer, which divide the Indus Valley from Zanskar and last, but not least of Leh. Don't take photographs looking back towards Leh because the airport, between the monastery and Leh, is classified as a military object. From Paldan Lamo Temple, on the peak of the mountain, a small path leads past a red Latho to the monastery proper. The built-in Dukhang is well worth seeing.

The area around the wall paintings, with its tankas, prayer-flags, bookshelves and books, is well illuminated. In spite of this you need a strong flash to take pictures. Near the Dukhang there are several other chapels of which the new Chokhang is above some stairs. Here funeral ceremonies can be witnessed. Many of the small, old prayer rooms, the head lama's room, and the rooms of the monks are, unfortunately no longer shown to foreigners. They contain some wonderful wall paintings, tankas, silver chortens, Buddha figures, statues of other deities and hundreds of books but some thoughtless tourists took objects as souvenirs. From the level of the Dukhang 19 steps lead up to the inner courtyard with a flagpole around which, on the 28th and 29th days of the 11th month of the Tibetan calendar, (midwinter) the Spitok Gurstor is celebrated with mask dances. At this festival the 'Jelbagh' dance masks, like those hanging on the walls of the monastery, are no longer used but rather true-to-life representations. The monastery has a statue of Kali whose face is only shown once a year.

Phyang (or Fiang) (16 km from Leh towards Srinagar, entrance fee Rs 10)
An access road leads to the monastery to the right of the main road. Phyang village is in the river valley, a few hundred metres walk away. Again you must take care when photographing — the barren mountain side opposite Phyang is a military zone! Phyang Lake, to the north of the gompa, is in a restricted area and therefore off limits. The Phyang Gompa has 50 lamas and seven 'novices' of the red-cap sect and possesses five chapels. The 650 year old Dukhang Temple was renovated in the late '70s.

An important religious festival with mask dances is celebrated on the 18th day of the first month of the Tibetan calendar. If you go down into the village from the monastery or the main road you may be able to see a wonderful kitchen in a Phyang farmhouse. The summer kitchen in the upper

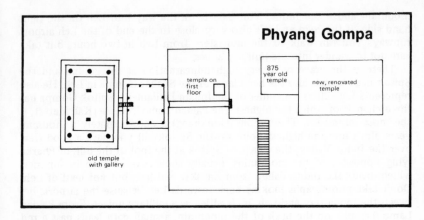

Phyang Gompa

875 year old temple

new, renovated temple

temple on first floor

old temple with gallery

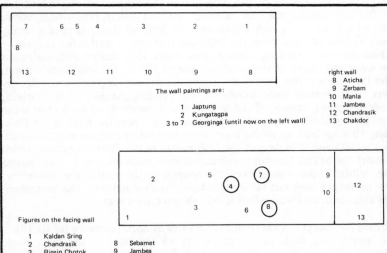

```
7        6  5   4        3           2              1

8

13       12     11      10        9          8
```

right wall
8 Aticha
9 Zerbam
10 Manla
11 Jambea
12 Chandrasik
13 Chakdor

The wall paintings are:

1 Japtung
2 Kungatagpa
3 to 7 Georginga (until now on the left wall)

```
        2        5     7                    9
                 4                          10

        3           6   8                   12

1                                           13
```

Figures on the facing wall

1 Kaldan Sring
2 Chandrasik
3 Rigsin Chotok
4 Chigten Gonbo
5 Chisger Tuba
6 Chisger Tuba
7 Nambar Namsat
8 Sebamet
9 Jambea
10 Dorje Zemba
11 Padme Gelsan
12 Chamba
13 Chchgi Garsen

The figures in the old temple of Phyang are, from left to right:

1 Choje Tamchosh Gurma, an early head lama of Phyang
2 Darma Kunga Tagpa
3 Tilasanpo
4 Chandrasik with three small figures
5 500 year old smaller Buddha to the left, near the pictures of the late head lama
6 Darje Chang, left before the faded 1900 year old small figure of Tuang Tonkerma
7 Padma Zamba
8 Chorje Gambopa
9 Skorba Rinpoche
10 Ranacheri
11 Chorten and to the right, in the corcorner, Chandrasik

storey is so lavishly equipped with dishes inherited over the generations that you feel like you are in a living museum. The sturdily built farmhouses generally have three storeys. The stables and storerooms are found on the ground floor. Above these is the so-called 'winter kitchen', which also serves as the living and sleeping room for the entire family during the winter. These close living arrangements, plus 'floor heating' from the stables beneath, conserves precious fuel (usually wood or dried cattle dung). A small animal may also be kept in this collective living room over the winter.

In the summer the family moves up to the top storey, which is often just a summer kitchen set on the roof. They sleep under the stars in summer. In Leh you may also see houses on whose roofs groundsheets are spread out, under which the house owners live, as if they were camping in tents. The summer night temperatures are low enough to make westerners reach for their sleeping bags, but they don't bother the Ladakhis at all. They're a hardy race! At a festival in Bodh Kharbu we saw a cook who, in the absence of a drinking vessel, took a draught of boiling butter tea in his cupped hands and drank from that as if it had been no more than a handful of cold water. Rich farmhouses will have special drinking vessels for butter tea or chang.

Beacon Highway
The Beacon Highway leads from Leh into the Nubra Valley over a pass at

view from Phyang Gompa

5606 metres — making it probably the highest road in the world. 'You can have dialogue with God' according to the road builder's sign! Only in September and October is the road open, at other times ice covers the road on the northern side of the Nubra Valley. For foreigners the road is closed year round since the Nubra Valley is in the restricted area and can only be visited with special permission.

Tibetan Refugee Camp

Near Choglamsar, on the left side of the Leh-Shey road, about nine km from Leh and close to the Indus, is the Sonam Ling refugee camp. More than 2000 refugees have lived here, under the most primitive conditions, since the early '60s. They have managed to grow some vegetables on this rocky ground but live mainly on the donations of international aid organisations,

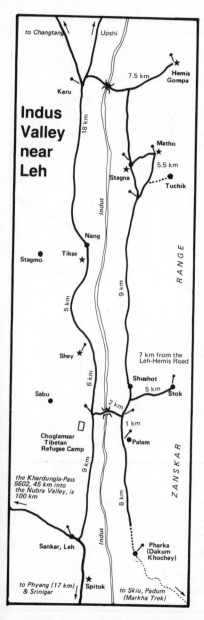

Indus Valley near Leh

to Changtang

Upshi

Karu

7.5 km

Hemis Gompa

18 km

Indus

Matho

5.5 km

Stagna

Tuchik

Nang

Stagmo

Tikse

5 km

9 km

RANGE

Shey

6 km

7 km from the Leh-Hemis Road

Shushot

5 km

Stok

Sabu

2 km

1 km

Choglamsar Tibetan Refugee Camp

Palam

9 km

ZANSKAR

the Khardungla-Pass 5602, 45 km into the Nubra Valley, is 100 km

8 km

Indus

Sankar, Leh

Pharka (Dakum Khochey)

to Phyang (17 km) & Srinigar

Spitok

to Skiu, Padum (Markha Trek)

having had to come to terms with the change from the mountain heights to the banks of the Indus. They also earn some money from handicrafts, particularly the manufacture of Tibetan carpets. The Tibetans are known as fair dealers and have only slowly infiltrated the Kashmiri dominated artifacts business in Ladakh.

Choglamsar is the main training place for Buddhist monks in Ladakh. Since the Chinese invasion of Tibet the philosophy school, on the right-hand side of the road from Leh to Hemis, has become an important centre for the study of Tibetan literature and history and of Buddhist philosophy in its pure form. Many westerners, interested in Buddhist learning and meditation, have also studied here. Choglamsar has an extensive syllabus and its library is worth seeing, even for the casual visitor.

In 1977 the old bridge at Sonam Ling was replaced with a new one able to take heavy vehicles. There are mani-stones in the village of Palam (across the road and turn right) which has a mixed Buddhist and Moslem population. The Hemis-Stagna-Palam road is very rough and there are some river crossings to be made but there is a regular bus connection.

Shey (15 km from Leh towards Hemis, entrance fee Rs 5)

The old 'summer palace' of the kings of Ladakh was built about 550 years ago. It stands next to the remains of a larger construction on the east side of a hill which runs south-east towards the Indus. From

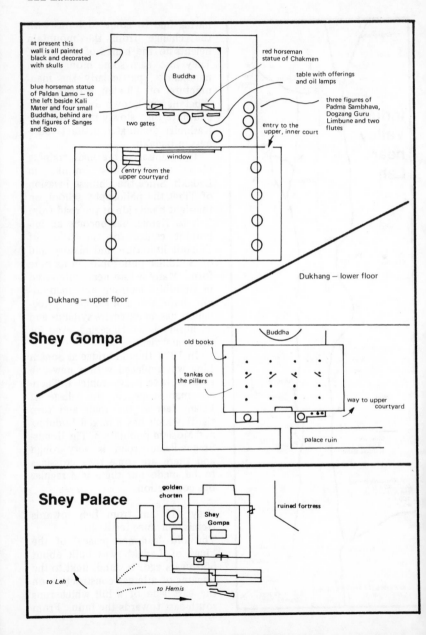

at present this wall is all painted black and decorated with skulls

Buddha

red horseman statue of Chakmen

table with offerings and oil lamps

three figures of Padma Sambhava, Dogzang Guru Limbune and two flutes

blue horseman statue of Paldan Lamo — to the left beside Kali Mater and four small Buddhas, behind are the figures of Sanges and Sato

two gates

entry to the upper, inner court

window

entry from the upper courtyard

Dukhang — lower floor

Dukhang — upper floor

Shey Gompa

Buddha

old books

tankas on the pillars

way to upper courtyard

palace ruin

Shey Palace

golden chorten

Shey Gompa

ruined fortress

to Leh

to Hemis

the palace you can see over the fertile Indus plain north-east to the Tikse Gompa and over the Indus to the Zanskar mountain range. Hundreds of chortens of the most diverse forms and sizes stand on the barren plains to the north, separated from the fertile river bank land by the Hemis road.

The old Shey palace has the largest golden Buddha statue in Ladakh in its gompa. The statue is worked out of gold and gilded copper sheets, stands 12 metres high and has blue hair. It was erected by King Dalden Namgyal in the middle of the 17th century. Sacrificial offerings (grain, jewels), holy signs and mantras are contained inside the figure. The most important moment in the construction of such a figure is when the eyes are painted in and the statue can 'see'. No artist or monk would dare to look the Buddha in the eye so the pupils are painted over the artist's shoulder, with his back to the idol.

In July the Metukba festival takes place in the Shey Gompa with one day of prayers for the well being of all life in the entire world. The upper chapel (Dukhang-Chung) of the Shey Gompa is used for everyday functions, it surrounds the Buddha figure's head as a sort of balcony. The lower, somewhat larger, chapel houses a large collections of tankas and a library. All the old tankas bear the stamp of the 'Gompa Association, Ladakh'.

The best time to visit the Shey Gompa is between 7 and 9 am or 5 and 6 pm since the monks perform their prayer-devotions at these times. The gompa is usually closed to the public at other times. In that event, the monk Tashi, whom you can find in the small village before Shey, will know where to find the key.

Shey Oracle

As in Mulbekh, Tikse, Matho, Stok and other Ladakh villages, Shey has an oracle. During the Shey Shublas, the August harvest festival, the Shey oracle rides on a horse and stops at various places around Shey to prophesy the future. The oracle, a Shey layman, starts at the Tuba Gompa where he engages in a two or three-day prayer, while in a trance, in order to be possessed and become an oracle. The Shey oracle is held in the highest regard and viewed as a God who has achieved the highest level of existence. Other oracles, especially those in Tikse and Stok, are not so well regarded but are at the same time feared and revered because of their spiritual state. It is said that if one asks a question of an oracle but disbelieves the answer and goes to another oracle, no anwer will be given.

Tikse Gompa (17 km from Leh towards Hemis, entrance fee Rs 10)

The Tikse monastery, perched on a hill high above the Indus, has the largest contingent of monks in Ladakh and its new found tourist wealth is being put to good use in some major improvements and renovations. About one hundred yellow-cap monks belong to the gompa. If you get there by 6.30

Wallpaintings in the high prayer room of Tikse Gompa:

left   right
1 Gonbo Ping   1 Chamsing
2 Gonbo Chakjipac   2 Lamo
3 Gonbo Chhak Tukpa   3 Chosgialckhor
4 Gonkar
5 Sangdu

```
        ┌──────────────────────┬──────────────────┐
        5    4    3    2    1   ↓   1    2    3
```

Figures:
Flag pole (Gyaltsan) in the middle, to the right of Chosgial,
left of Tsepakmet.

In the prayer room there are two seats, one for the Dali
Lama who visited Tikse in 1973 and 1976, and one for the
head lama of Tikse

Behind the prayer room:

1 Sharipu
2 Buddha
3 Mongalpu
4 Shikdan and Chamsing
5 Chandajik

```
┌───────────────────────────────────────┐
│                                        │
│   (1)    (2)    (3)      ┌───┐          │
│                         │(4)│  (5)     │
└─────────────────────────┴───┴──────────┘
```

Zan La Temple
at Tikse

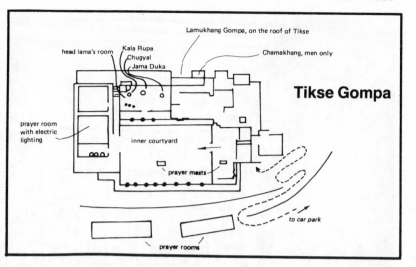

Lamukhang Gompa, on the roof of Tikse

Chamakhang, men only

head lama's room

Kala Rupa

Chugyal

Jama Duka

Tikse Gompa

prayer room
with electric
lighting

inner courtyard

prayer masts

to car park

prayer rooms

am you can witness the daily morning prayers but there are also prayers closer to noon, preceded by long, mournful sounds from the horns on the roof. The monastery mountain is best ascended on foot although there is also a new 1.5 km sealed road up to the monastery.

The small temple of Zan-La is beside the car parking area on this road. In the gompa courtyard there are some interesting Tibetan calendars on the walls. In the chapel there is a picture, near the central Chamba statue, of Tsung-Khapas, the founder of the Tugend (Gelugpa) sect. Some steps run up to a roof balcony from which there is access to the rooms of the head lama. Above everything is the roof top Lamukhang chapel, to which the Chamakhang also belongs, where only men may go. If you remain very quiet you may also see the mice nibbling at the offerings of grain and drinking the water. Whereas a few years ago travellers could buy, for a few rupees at the most, a printed prayer flag, today the monks wait in the monastery yard with portable stands from which they sell monastic souvenirs!

Below the monastery there are further chapels which are not very attractive. The 'houses' of the monks stretch out towards the foot of the hill. Tikse has an important festival with mask dances, the Tikse Gurstor, on the 18th and 19th day of the 12th month of the Tibetan calendar.

When asked what criteria are used to choose lamas, or which sons in a family will become monks, a monk of Tikse told us that he came from a family with four sons. His eldest brother is a farmer, the second eldest is a teacher and his youngest brother a monk like himself. In principle all could become monks but the father must give his consent. This he will certainly not give to all his sons because some must stay on to run the farm and look after the rest of the family.

library at Tikse Gompa

Tikse Oracle
The Tikse oracle is the most important oracle in Ladakh. An old man in the
village is supposed to have supernatural powers. In a trance this layman, for
he is not a lama, is possessed by a spirit and speaks Tibetan, a language
which he cannot normally understand. He is said to be able to perform mir-
aculous cures on beasts and men. With the help of a small tube he can 'suck'
diseases from the bodies of the ill. He also gives advice for healing and can
predict the future. In 1975 a new oracle appeared, the young wife of a Leh
carpenter. Even in her youth there were special indications of her status as
an oracle.

Printing
Tikse Gompa possesses a rich and beautiful library with many hand-written
or painted books. Recent editions are produced by block printing, as in old
Tibet. This procedure is also used today for the printing of the holy books
Kandshur, Tibetan gka-hgyur, 'the translated word' of Buddha and Tand-
shur, 'the translated teachings' of the Lamaist religious teachers Bu-Ston
(1290-1364 AD). The latter consists of a 225 volume commentary on the
Kandshur! Wooden printing plates are made up for each page and pressed by
hand. The many hundred volumes indicate how much space the printing
plates must take up in the monastery. Older and more highly regarded editions are often printed not black on white but painted with gold ink on black

lacquered paper. These are decorated with Buddha figures. The individual pages are not bound up but kept as collections of loose sheets, wrapped in cloth between two wooden boards, tied up with a strap and stored on the shelves. Tikse Gompa has the most beautiful library. In Hemis Gompa there are some rarities such as bilingual books in Tibetan and Sanskrit. You may meet one of the porters who has to lug the heavy books from the gompa to a village for a festival — the monks themselves follow on much later.

above: porter carrying books

above right: pages from a book

Hemis Gompa (45 km from Leh, entrance fee Rs 10)
Hemis is easily reached by car or jeep from Leh but rather difficult to get to
by public transport. By car you follow the Upshi road past Shey and Tikse,
this is the Manali road which follows the Indus. Past the TCP checkpoint at
Karu you turn to the right to cross the Indus over a new bridge and follow
the winding road up towards the gompa. Unlike many other gompas Hemis
is not visible from afar — it only comes into view when you're right beside
it.

There is only one regular bus a day from Leh towards Hemis and it does
not go right to the gompa. You take the Sakti bus which departs Leh
around 11 am and get down at Karu bridge. You then have to walk up the
six km road, it takes about two hours. Since the bus continues on to Sakti,
turns around there and starts off on the return trip to Leh at 2 or 2.30 pm
there is no way you can get up to the gompa and back down to catch the
bus back on the same day. Thus if you want to visit Hemis by bus you must
plan on staying overnight at the monastery and returning the next day. During the tourist season the tourist office erects tents at Hemis for overnight
visitors.

The gompa is famous far beyond the borders of Ladakh for its Hemis
Festival (Hemis Setchu or Mela of the Hemis Gompa). This takes place every
year with mask dances on the 10th and 11th day of the fifth Tibetan
month. This date usually falls in the second half of June although it sometimes goes into the beginning of July. Hemis also has a gigantic tanka, one
of the largest in the world, which is only displayed to the public every 11
years at the Hemis Festival. It was unveiled at the 1980 festival so it will not
be shown again until 1991. The festival draws pilgrims from all over Ladakh
and, since 1975, tourists from all over the world. Apart from being one of
the largest in Ladakh it is virtually the only major religious festival in
Ladakh which is held in the summer, when the passes are open. A monastery in Zanskar has a similar festival, with mask dances, in the summer
months. Recently there have been deliberations by the monks of Karsha
Gompa, the Zanskar monastery near Padum, whether mask dances usually
held in the winter months should be switched to the summer. This would be
a further attraction for a visit to Zanskar.

Hemis Gompa is one of the most important in Ladakh quite apart from
its annual festival. You can gain an impression of the extent of the monastery area by climbing the so called eyrie, a hermitage (Gotsang Gompa)
reached by a one hour, three km climb to 3900 metres. The 13th century
monastery pre-dates the Hemis Gompa and was built by Syalwa Gotsang-

A Crossing the Himalayas, Kun and Nun below, from
    Srinagar to Leh
B Window shopping in Leh
C Leh's main street

Pa. There are about a dozen monks living there.

The thousand square metre courtyard of the Hemis Gompa is entered from the north-east. The two prayer flags, in front of the first steps up to the Dukhang, form the middle point during the mask dances. To the left there is a gallery, from which there is a good view of the dancers during the festival. A few places are reserved for guests but it is sometimes possible to buy 'admission tickets' to the gallery from business-minded monks! The day before the two-day festival proper is devoted to demonstrations. On the first day of the festival the part which foreigners can watch begins at 10 am with ceremonies in the courtyard. After prayers in the Dukhang the Rimpoche climbs the steps up to the courtyard, accompanied by musician monks, crosses it and takes his place underneath the gallery.

Shortly afterwards the dances begin, which have as their theme the struggle against evil and infidels and the inevitable victory of good and of Buddhism. The Padmasambhavas dance, which shows the conquest of the Ruta demons, is part of this dance. Other figures which the dancers represent are Yama — the God of Death, the black-hatted sorcerer Guru Trakpo — the vanquisher of all demons, and various other forms of Padmasambhavas. The sequence of the dances changes with time — often to present a different finale for the benefit of distinguished guests! The dancing continues to late afternoon, with a brief stop at mid-day. Locals and foreigners find time to patronise the many small stands outside the monastery walls where tea, soup, tsampa, sweets and other refreshments are sold. If you wish to take photographs take account of the position of the sun when selecting your vantage point. In the crowded conditions during the dancing it is virtually impossible to leave your place.

If you visit the gompa outside the festival time you will be impressed by the stillness of the valley. You will also have the opportunity to see the various chapels. Near the Dukhang is the Lakhang, which is the first one after a small set of steps from the yard. The doors are placed inwards so that the front room stands behind, its roof supported with four poles. The side walls of this front room are covered with partially damaged frescoes of the watchers of the heavenly directions. In the Dukhang, the general assembly room, the throne of the Rimpoche dominates the sitting places of the monks. In the Lakhang there is a large gilded statue of the Buddha Shakimuni with blue hair, surrounded by several silver chortens which, as in Spitok Gompa, are decorated with semi precious stones. There are also beautiful frescoes on the Lakhang Nyingpa which is otherwise practically empty. The hands of the artists who prepared the gompa's giant tanka are

A   In the back streets of Leh
B   Monk in Spitok Gompa
C   Wall painting in Shergol Gompa

revered as holy relics but Hemis also has many lesser, but still interesting, tankas. Hemis also has an excellent library, particularly well preserved wall paintings and good Buddha figures.

In the second and third storeys, near the other chapels like the Zankhang, there is the Kharrabgysal, the rooms of the Rimpoche or head lama. The Rimpoche, spiritual overlord of Hemis, is a reincarnation of the monastery's founder, Stagtshang Raspa, who built Hemis in the first half of the 17th century, under King Sengge Namgyal who also established the monasteries of Chemre, Hanle and Tmosgang. The last overlord of the gompa was a reincarnation who, as a five-year old child, was undergoing training in Tibet when the Chinese invaded. Since then the Chakzot (manager) a brother of the late king of Ladakh, has conducted the business of the gompa. Because of the Chinese takeover of Tibet the monastery has had no communication with its Rimpoche since the '60s. During the 1975 festival Drugpa Rimpoche, a 12 year-old youth, became the new Rimpoche as a new incarnation.

He is at the same time the overlord of the Drugpa Kargyupa, one of the six divisions of the red-cap sect who, before the Chinese invasion of Tibet, possessed influence practically only in Bhutan and Ladakh. In Ladakh the Stagna and

top: Hemis Gompa

bottom: spectators at the Hemis festival

Chemre monasteries belong to this order, while Spitok belongs to the yellow-cap (Gelugpa order). Drugpa Rimpoche currently lives in Darjeeling, where he is completing his training.

Festivals

Although the great religious festivals of Ladakh almost all fall in the winter, practically all the villages have harvest thanksgiving festivals and archery events during the summer. There are also private parties in which dance plays an important role. In these slow, sustained dances the dancers appear to be between dream and trance. Many of the dances, which have a musical accompaniment of drums and flutes, show interesting elements from the daily life of farmers. Hand movements, for example, are unmistakeably taken from the actions involved in sowing seeds. In general men and women dance totally separately. If they are together on the same 'dance floor' they will still do their own, unrelated, dances. We experienced a special feature during a celebration at Bodh Kharbu — a dance master selected from the crowd some women and young girls to dance. After initial reluctance they seemed to quite enjoy it.

Ladakhi archery contests, which are followed by more dancing, are only a pale reflection of similar festivals in other Himalayan states. Whereas in Bhutan specially design-

top & bottom: dancers
at the Hemis festival

ed and fashioned bows would be used for such a contest, in Ladakh the bows are much cruder. Nevertheless these contests have their own charm and they do give you the opportunity to see the making of chang, butter-tea and tsampa. No matter what else happens at a festival these three ingredients must be included. Festival musicians are generally paid in local produce. After a good meal they receive, with their cup of butter-tea, a cup of tsampa meal, sometimes also sugar and a piece of butter. The whole lot is wrapped up in a piece of cloth and knotted for transport.

Anyone wishing to tape record festival music should keep their microphone concealed. Otherwise all that will result is a wild medley of noises since the Ladakhis are fascinated by these strange technological instruments. They will point it out to the audience and comment loudly! A cassette recorder with an inbuilt microphone can be kept out of sight, even inside a carrying bag.

Chemre Gompa
If you turn to the left at the Karu TCP you will, after five km, reach Chemre Gompa on a ridge above the village of Chemre. Like Hemis it was founded by Stagtshang Raspa but in contrast to Hemis the mask dances are held at the turn of the year in the Tibetan calendar — in mid-winter. The Dukhang and the three further chapels above it are not really worth visiting. The small, but noteworthy, Trak Tok Gompa is 10 km further on. The old Trak Tok Rimpoche, who came from Tibet, is highly revered by the Ladakhis. The old cave-chapel, which is reminiscent of Dakum Khochey, is especially interesting. Although they both lie in a restricted zone tourists may visit the Chemre and Trak Tok Gompas.

Leh-Manali Road
At the Upshi TCP (a km before Upshi) the road deviates to the right, crosses a pioneer bridge across the Indus, and turns into a side valley. Up to the Upshi TCP no special documentation is required but from here on special permission is needed from the District Commissioner in Leh. The Leh-Manali road is 475 km long and is only recommended for fully equipped four-wheel drives since no refuelling or repair facilities are available. The road is normally open only in September and October, the highest pass is the Tanglang La (5429 metres), 65 km beyond Upshi. There is no public transport along this stretch although in summer there is a bus service from Keylong to Manali, a distance of about 117 km crossing the Rohtang Pass. Two km before Miru a line of mani-pennants spans the whole valley.

Hemis to Leh on the other side of the Indus
The Hemis-Stagna-Choglamsar road on the left bank of the Indus is sealed for a short distance but was badly damaged in 1978 due to unusually severe weather.

Matho Gompa

Matho lies five km from Stagna in a southern side valley. The monastery is above the village with many grain mills, on a long ridge surrounded by a small forest. The gompa was founded in the 16th century by Tungpa Dorje and today it has 60 monks and 30 novices from the larger monasteries. It belongs to the Sakyapa sect. Near the chapels, which were renovated for the visit of Sakya Trinzin Rimpoche, overlord of the sect, is a small room which is very interesting. This room, called Gonkhang, is filled 50 cm high with grain. According to an old custom every family from Matho brings a small bowl of grain from the first harvest for this room. This is not accompanied by any special ceremony. There is a lama who is particularly responsible for the Gonkhang room; he is changed every three years. The room has a special significance during the two-day Nagrang Festival (at the Tibetan New Year, in February) and a one-day festival on the 8th day of the second Tibetan month (usually March) called the Nispetsergyat.

During these two festivals two special monks (called Rongzam) go into a trance in this room and then, adorned with old weapons, run over the mountain ridges in the area and over the roofs of the monastery. During the Nagrang Festival the lamas are evil-minded on the first day (they hit spectators) but very peacable on the second day. At the Nespetsergyat these two Rongzam ride the stretch which they went over on foot at the beginning of the Tibetan year. Both of these festivals are accompanied by mask dances. For these two monks, there stand two red chortens of a special style, called Lhato, from which prayer flags flutter. They are situated high in the mountains, about five or six km from the monastery, close to a glacier. The monks, also known as Luyar, are just like other monks at other times of the year, but if someone in the village doesn't believe in or has lost faith in the powers of Buddhism, these two monks batter themselves on the arms, feet and tongue with their old weapons. The wounds do not bleed and their injuries heal so quickly that they are able to dance a short time later. They do this in order to show that they possess divine powers. This ritual is still practised today on the 14th and 15th days of the first month of the Tibetan calendar. Like the monks of the Gonkhang room they are replaced every three years, the choice is made, following a prayer, from four or five candidates. All 60 monks write the name of their candidates on a small piece of paper. The head lama draws two of these pieces of paper out and those are the monks for the next three years.

In front of the door to the Gonkhang room there is a prayer mill made out of oil cans — a sign of the times, but still adorned with the

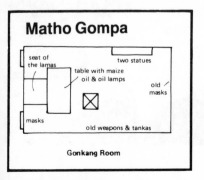

Matho Gompa

seat of the lamas

two statues

table with maize oil & oil lamps

old masks

masks

old weapons & tankas

Gonkang Room

elderly pilgrim at a gompa

mantra 'Om mani padme hum' in addition to other prayers. They are written on a paper roll, not on little scraps of paper. The Gonkhang room, in which meditation takes place, is ascribed its own spiritual power. Thus one cannot in any circumstances take photographs here because pictures of the room would take away a part of the power.

Matho is famous, at least amongst Ladakhis, because of its oracle. The Lhaba of Matho is, in contrast to the oracle of Tikse, a priest and lives in the monastery. On special days (in winter on the 8th day of the second month of the Tibetan calendar) the oracle runs all over the mountains near Matho, blindfolded and 'sees' only with a painting on breast and back. The oracle speaks to the audience of village dwellers by a small spring at the foot of the monastery mountain.

Stagna Gompa

This gompa lies on a sugarloaf mountain in the Indus Valley. It cannot be reached directly from the Leh-Hemis road because there is no bridge, one must use the Choglamsar or Karu bridge. In the chapel there are three new paintings — a large picture of Choshikzal, the red figure of Standin and the blue figure of Dorje Chang. In the wooden cupboard there is a large standing figure of Dorje Phakma besides eight Sashan Gyat. Under this major chapel there is another chapel which may only be entered by lamas. Stagna has 25 red-cap monks and the head lama can offer his visitors a European sofa with two easy chairs — of which he is more than a little proud.

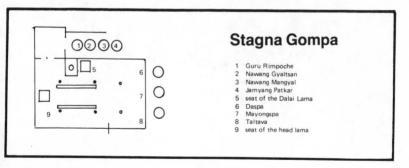

Stagna Gompa

1 Guru Rimpoche
2 Nawang Gyaltsan
3 Nawang Mangyal
4 Jamyang Patkar
5 seat of the Dalai Lama
6 Daspa
7 Mayongspa
8 Taltava
9 seat of the head lama

Stok Palace

Eight km towards the Indus from Stagna, then four km over a rubble slope at the outlet of a side valley, will bring you to the palace of Stok. Coming from Leh you cross the Indus at Choglamsar then travel a km towards the Indus and turn to the right. The palace is about 200 years old and is the only Ladakhi royal palace which is still inhabited. The last king, Rajah Kunsang Namgyal, died in 1974 and, as is customary for personalities of high standing, a chorten was erected in the village where he was cremated. One of

royal palace at Stok

his brothers is now the 'manager' of the Hemis gompa but only his widow, the Rani of Stok, and his youngest son live in the palace. The widow, who was formerly revered as the Gyalmo, Rani Parvati Davi Deskit Wangmo, the 18th Queen of Ladakh, was born in 1936. She has four children — the eldest son will become the next King of Ladakh when he is 20 to 25 years old. The exact date will be set by lamas and people of high standing. Gyalpo means king, Gyalmo is queen, Gyallu is prince, Gyalmo Chhunun is princess.

The palace of Stok has 80 rooms, only 12 of which are now used. There are 25 servants working for the Rani but because the palace is so difficult to heat the Rani moves south to Manali for the winter months. The King of Ladakh formerly had a cabinet of five ministers and the influence of Ladakh's kings once reached from Demchok (on the present day Chinese-Tibetan border) to Mulbekh and in the north over the Nubra Valley. Today the political power rests with the Indian governor, the District Commissioner. Apart from the palace Stok's only other attraction is the July archery contest. As in Matho you can see the small water mills in which the roasted grain is ground into meal. There are two lay oracles in Stok and they give their 'performance' at the Lchagrang Festival on the 9th and 10th days of the third month of the Tibetan calendar.

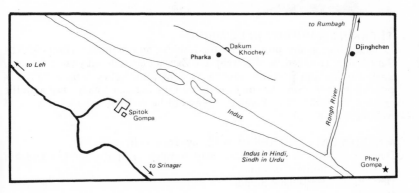

Pharka

The village of Pharka is on the opposite side of the Indus from, and in sight of, the Spitok Gompa. You can only reach Pharka by the Choglamsar route, the last kms must be made on foot but up to that point the road is jeepable. At the village of Pharka there is a cave in the sandstone bank of the Indus. The cave gompa was built by Lotsava Ringchen Sanghpo and is older than Spitok Gompa. In front of the gompa cave there is a building housing a small primary school. The teacher enjoys painting 'modern' tankas in his spare time.

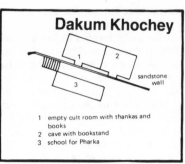

1 empty cult room with thankas and
   books
2 cave with bookstand
3 school for Pharka

a Ladakhi child

TREKKING & MOUNTAIN CLIMBING
Ladakh offers many possibilities for trekking and mountain climbing. The
Suru Valley (reached from Kargil) and Zanskar are especially good for trekking. Zanskar can only be reached over the Suru Valley from Kargil; it is
possible to trek from Nimmu directly into the Zanskar Valley only with the
greatest difficulty. The Zanskar Valley can be reached in about a week of
walking from Kargil.

MARKHA VALLEY TREK (9 to 12 days from Leh)
Day 1:   Bus or taxi to Karu, stay overnight in Martseland in a Ladakhi
            house if possible.
Day 2:   Martseland-Sumdo
Day 3:   Sumdo-Chokdo
Day 4:   Chokdo-Larsa
Day 5:   Larsa-Nimaling over a 5200 metre pass
Day 6:   Nimaling-Hankar
Day 7:   Hankar-Omlud
Day 8:   Omlud-Markha Gompa, this is the start of the route to Zangla
            in Zanskar
Day 9:   Markha Gompa-Skiu
Day 10:   Skiu-Shingo
Day 11:   Shingo-Rumbagh, over the Ganda Pass
Day 12:   Rumbagh-Leh, over the Namlung Pass

LEH-MARKHA VALLEY-ZANGLA (ZANSKAR)-PADUM
See the Zanskar section under Padum-Leh Trek

LEH—KONGLACHA PEAK
The Konglacha Peak, (6700 metres) lies south-east of Leh.

Day 1:   Leh-Stok
Day 2:   Hiring of porters and ponies in Stok, prices are fixed by the Labour Office.
Day 3:   From Stok, past the Kurphuk Gompa above Stok and on to the Namlung Pass on foot.
Day 4:   Cross the 4880 metre Namlung Pass.
Day 5:   To Rumbagh, a village at 3270 metres.
Day 6:   To the base camp of Konglacha Peak, it takes a further two days to climb the peak.

LEH-KOCHTET PEAK
The Kochtet Peak (7015 metres) is in the restricted zone. From Leh to Changla is 79 km along a jeepable road. You leave Leh on the Indus road to Hemis Gompa. At Karu you turn left into the restricted zone. The ascent takes four days. Note that north of the Srinagar-Leh road and east of the Leh-Manali road is a restricted area so all treks must be confined to the other side of these roads. You should be well-equipped with mountaineering rations.

LEH-SIHUMAR
This trek takes eight to nine days over Shang.

LEH-MANALI
Before setting out on this 14 day trek you must obtain a permit from the DC in Leh. Otherwise your trek will come to an end at the control post before Upshi. You follow the Indus Valley as far as Upshi where you turn into a side valley over the Miru, Gya and the Tanglang La Pass to Rukchen. Then it is over the Marangla Pass, past Sutak, over the Lachalang La (5070 metres) and the Baralacha Pass (4938 metres) and through Darcha to Keylong. Finally you cross the Rohtang Pass to Manali.

ALCHI-CHILING SUMDA
A four day trek.

KARGIL-MANALI TREK
See the Zanskar section.

opposite page — looking over Leh with the Leh Palace in the background.

above — school for monks in Lekir Gompa

left — young schoolgirl in Pharka

MOUNTAIN CLIMBING

Ladakh was practically shut off from the outside world between the end of WW II and 1974 so the mountaineer will find many 5000 to 7000 metre peaks which have not yet been climbed. Some have not even been named. Since the Ladakh valleys are at altitudes of 3500 to 4000 metres the mountain ascents are only a thousand to 3000 metres. The 1980s are likely to see a large influx of western mountaineering enthusiasts. Japanese teams have already started conquering some of these virgin peaks.

MAIN HIMALAYAN PEAKS
heights in metres

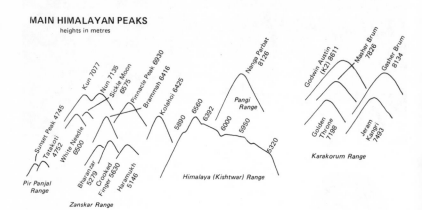

Kun 7077
Nun 7135
Sickle Moon 6575
Pinnacle Peak 6930
Brammah 6416
Kolahoi 6425
Nanga Parbat 8126
Godwin Austin (K2) 8611
Masher Brum 7826
Gasher Brum 8134
Sunset Peak 4745
Tatakoti 4752
White Needle 6500
5890
6560
6392
Pangi Range
6000
5950
5320
Golden Throne 7198
Jeram Kangri 7493
Bharanzar 5279
Crooked Finger 5630
Haramukh 5146
Pir Panjal Range
Karakorum Range
Himalaya (Kishtwar) Range
Zanskar Range

Karakoram

The range of mountains north of Ladakh, and thus north of the Himalayas, has 10 peaks over 7000 metres including, at 8611 metres, the world's second highest peak, Mt Godwin Austen, also known as K2. It stands in the Pakistani held part of Kashmir. Because the mountains in the Karakoram rise from a base altitude averaging close to 3000 metres they do not look as impressive as the Himalayas.

Pir Panjal

This mountain range is south of the Himalayas. The Vale of Kashmir is between the Pir Panjals and the Himalayas. The Lahaul Valley, north of Manali and south of Ladakh, is similarly sandwiched between the two ranges.

Zanskar

Zanskar, the region between Kargil and Lamayuru in the north and Kisht-war and Manali in the south is, at the moment, an ideal trekking area. The new road from Kargil, over the Pensi La to Padum will bring a post office, bank and even a phone connection to the Zanskar capital but at present you will find none of these, or any hotels. Nor will you find military installations and soldiers, a common part of the scene in Ladakh. The most you'll come across is a mounted patrol or pony-caravan of the J&K Police. As for foreign visitors they are still few and far between in this far 'off the beaten track' Himalayan valley. The valley is about 300 km long and is unusual in that access is only by high passes from the sides. A unique feature of the Zanskar area is the twin peak of Nun and Kun.

TREKKING TIPS
Certain precautions will make a Zanskar trek an easier proposition:

Survival Anyone intending to trek in Zanskar should be completely outfitted in Srinagar or, at the latest, Kargil. Very little will be found in Padum and in the small villages along the trail it is not easy to buy even tsampa meal. If you have porters or pony-leaders you should ensure that they feed themselves. Most important you must take sufficient kerosene (and ensure the containers do not leak!) since there is very little fuel for burning.

Food Westerners should take along tinned meat and other food suitable for strenuous walking at altitudes from 3000 to 5000 metres. A larger group could take along a sheep as live meat. If you wish to (or have to) survive Zanskari style you should bring tsampa (roasted grain) with tea, water and chang. A kind of noodle known as pakthuk can be prepared for a change and tsampa can also be baked as a flat bread called takir or, in Tibetan, pakleb. Chuli pak is a real Zanskari appetiser — it consists of apricots (chuli) cooked in butter (hopefully not rancid), which is then eaten with flat bread for breakfast.

Packing Clothing and equipment should be packed in a rucksack or kitbag, the latter are easier to transport on pony back. Waterproof individual items by putting them in dustbags sealed with rubber loops.

Walking stick A sturdy stick is important, especially for crossing streams.

Shoes Light canvas running shoes with rubber soles are recommended for trekking; they dry quickly after crossing streams. In no circumstances try to cross streams or rivers barefoot.

Sun hat Take a sun hat but ensure it stays firmly in place or it will soon be blown away.

Chap stick Important if you want to avoid burnt, dry lips.

Sunglasses Very important in the high mountains — good quality and 85% filter factor.

Safety pins Have them on hand, not packed somewhere far away or where they could be lost in a fall.

Parka & sleeping bag Both should be good quality since the nights can get very cold.

Tents Make sure the tent is waterproof, some monsoon rains creep over the mountain barrier and bring heavy downpours.

Ponies for trekking Ponies are indispensable for riding and haulage in the Kashmir Valley, particularly on the Pahalgam-Amarnath trek, and in Ladakh, particularly on treks into Zanskar. Locally supplied saddles tend to be very uncomfortable — in Pahalgam they are often made of iron: hard, inflexible, awkward and with just a little leather on top. In the Suru Valley the saddles are all made of wood. In either case riding rapidly becomes impossible, but not only are the saddles a nightmare, the bridle and stirrups are equally bad. In fact stirrups are often completely lacking on Suru Valley and Zanskar ponies and the bridle may be simply a loose rope tied around the animal's neck. A tall westerner, with his legs reaching almost to the ground, looks like Don Quixote! The reason for this poor equipment is quite simple — apart from water crossings ponies are primarily used only as beasts of burden and rarely ridden. If you wish to use your own saddle it is not necessary to bring it with you since saddles are sold in the neighbourhood of the Shah Hamadan Mosque in Srinagar. They can easily be resold after you complete your pony trek.

In choosing a pony, if you should be so fortunate as to have a choice, considering the limited number available, pay close attention to the rear and withers. Otherwise you will have an uncomfortable time on horseback. Forget whatever you know about horses when viewing these animals — they fly in the face of our preconceptions and are unbelievably nimble and surefooted. If you decide to entrust yourself to such a 'disguised deer' do not try to steer them, they find their own way with remarkable certainty. If you do want to direct the pony with the reins (they do not seem to understand hints on the shanks) then give a gentle indication and allow one or two seconds reaction time. They're not machines with instantaneous reactions! Over-strenuous tugging at the reins leads to defensive resistance.

Allow the ponies sufficiently long rest stops and opportunities to relax. The animals don't always find enough food at overnight halting places (at least in Zanskar) so they are allowed to wander in search of food at night. Don't blame the horse-drivers if it takes some time to round them up in the morning. The mid-day stop should, if possible, be at a place where ponies can graze. Unload them at this time and remove the saddles, you will see the ponies roll on their backs to reduce the flatulence caused by the tight belly band. The pause should not be too short or, further down the trail, the docile beasts may suddenly decide to throw off their load or rider and settle down to some serious grazing. Bear in mind that the smell of westerners is still unusual to Zanskari horses. A local horse-leader can be very reassuring for the ponies but if you ride alone it is important to tether your pony during stops. Otherwise it will gallop off home at the first opportunity.

The lightly tinkling bells found around the neck of Zanskari horses drown out the noise of falling stones and reassure the horses. Despite such precautions against panic horses do sometimes fall, as happened on our trek from Zangla to Nerag (see Padum-Lamayuru Trek) when our horse was drowned. This is naturally seen as a bad omen for the trip and porters and horse-drivers may desert you after such an accident. Financial compensation for the dead animal will help, it is often the horse-driver's sole possession. You must reckon on Rs 1000 to 2000. In general Zanskari horses and porters are more reliable than those from Kashmir. For horses from the Suru Valley the rope suspension bridges at Padum constitute an insurmountable obstacle on a trek to Zanskar and you will have to switch to Zanskari horses from Thonde or Zangla. They are able to get across these frightening bridges. Many porters from the Kashmir Valley are unwilling to go beyond Padum since they are unused to the high altitude passes (5000 metres) on the trek to Lamayuru, Leh or Manali.

RELIGIOUS FESTIVALS IN ZANSKAR

Karsha Gompa Gostor on the 25th-29th days of the 11th month of the Tibetan calendar — usually in the first week in January. Features cham dance with masks.

Tonde (Stongde) Gompa Gostor from the 29th day of the 11th month of the Tibetan calendar, it follows the end of the Karsha Gostor.

Bardan Gompa Gertsa on the 15th day of the fourth month (usually the first week in June), features cham dance with masks. This is the only Zanskar festival that takes place in the summer, the Hemis festival in Ladakh takes place at the same time and is similarly the only Ladakh summer festival.

Zongkhul Gompa Zongkhul Huchot takes place on the 16th and 17th days of the fourth month but there are no mask dances.

Sani Gompa Nungnes does not have a fixed date but usually takes place in July.

Sani Gompa Sani Nasjal takes place between the 15th and 20th days of the sixth Tibetan month, usually the first week in August. The festival takes place during the blooming of the 'Guru Neropa Flower'.

Phuctal Gompa Gostor is on the 29th and 30th day of the 12th Tibetan month and features prayers but no mask dances.

Mune Gompa Anchog takes place on the 15th day of the 11th month and is, once again, only prayers.

Tagrimo Gompa A one day prayer festival takes place on the 29th day of the 11th month, at the same time as the Karsha Gostor.

Padum The Padum Hurim or Skurim is on the 28th and 29th days of the 10th month of the Tibetan calendar and features cham dances with masks.

Zangla The Zangla Hurim is on the 28th and 29th day of the 10th month (first week in December). On the 29th day there will be mask dances in front of the Zangla Palace.

Lingshot Gompa Monlam takes place on the 15th day of the first Tibetan month (February) and consists of prayers.

TREKS TO/FROM ZANSKAR

Zanskar is often pronounced as Zanhar and still appears on many maps as Zaskar — one of those Victorian-era errors which cartographers have perpetuated right down to the present. There are many routes leading in to Zanskar, despite the region's isolation. The two most used routes are those from Kargil and from Manali to Padum, the capital of Zanskar. Apart from the most frequently used routes there are others less well known.

PAHALGAM (Kashmir)-PANNIKAR (Suru Valley)

An eight-day trek described in the Kashmir section.

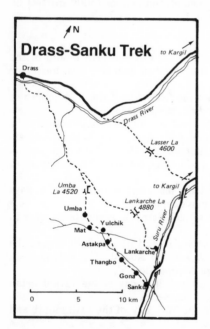

DRASS-SANKU TREK
(Suru Valley)

A three day trek from the Drass Valley directly into the Suru Valley, bypassing Kargil. It is suitable for a Zanskar trek, for a Drass-Sanku-Pannikar-Pahalgam trek or simply as a Drass-Sanku-Kargil mini-trek.

KARGIL-PADUM

After the completion of all bridges, (expected to be in 1981), especially those over the tributaries of the Stod in Zanskar, the Kargil-Padum road will be passable from early June to late-October. If the road between Namsuru and Parkachik is open and a vehicle is available then it is possible to go from Kargil to the Pensi La in one day and thus shorten the first four days of the trek detailed below to one.

Day 1: Kargil-Namsuru

The first day consists of preparation in Kargil then a bus or jeep trip to Namsuru. Beyond Kargil you do not follow the Leh road, which crosses the Suru at Chanchi over a metal bridge, but turn to the right into the Suru Valley. The route goes past the Hotel d'Zojila and leads over the 15 kms of already surfaced road over Grantung to the village of Rispong (20 km)

which has a mosque. The route continues past Martodas, Skininurai and Sanskritwe (Sanskarwe) to Sanku (Sankoo). Sanku is the end of the current bus route, 42 km out, and has a school and Dak Bungalow. The road switches to the right-hand side of the river four km past Sanku and continues for 7.5 km before changing back to the left-hand side towards Namsuru. From Sanku to Namsuru you pass through the villages of Kur, Phokra, Partik and Yoljok.

Day 2: Namsuru-Pannikar-Parkutse
Horses and porters can be hired in Namsuru or Pannikar but it is a good idea to book horses in advance as they may all be out on the trail. The road continues along the river valley but the trekking route cuts off the large river bend. The Suru River is crossed over a large wooden bridge near to Namsuru (3480 metres), the route then climbs over the town of Pannikar in zig-zag curves to a ridge, from which the Kun and Nun massif can be seen to the south-east.

Most of the horses hired in the Namsuru-Pannikar region for trekking in Zanskar will be hired from Kashmiris because this is where the last major settlement of Indo-Aryans and Moslems is to be found. Note that on the road to Pannikar roads marked 'impassable' may only be partially blocked by landslides and can be carefully crossed. Beyond the ridge of Pannikar

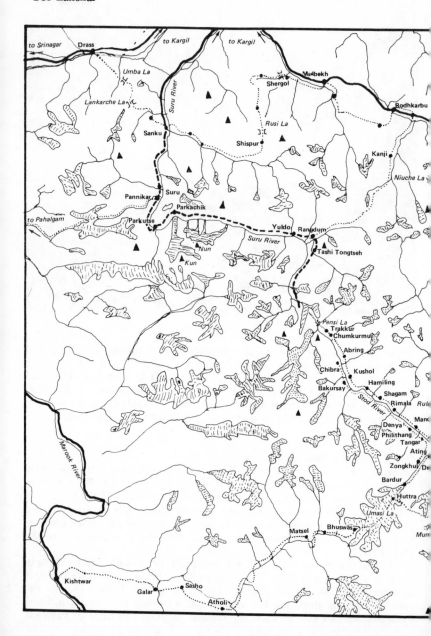

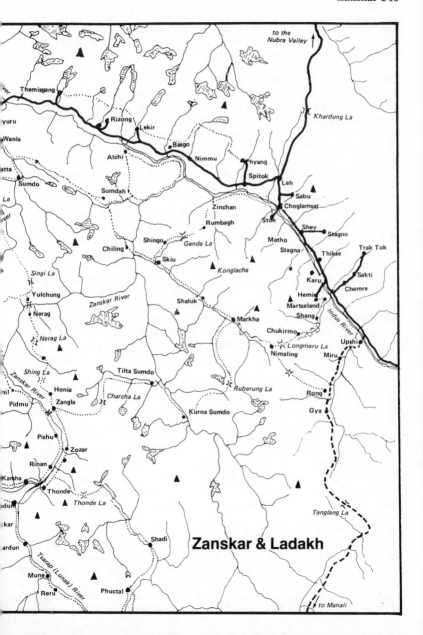

Zanskar & Ladakh

the trekking route winds down to a good camping spot with fresh grass at Parkutse. Here you meet the road again, from here to the Rangdum Gompa it runs along the northern river bank.

Day 3: Parkutse-Parkachik-Yuldo-Rangdum Gompa

Between the village of Parkachik and the next camping place at Gulmatang there is some absolutely breathtaking scenery in this practically uninhabited valley. On the other side of the river the Ganri glacier extends directly from the Nun and Kun saddle to the river below, it's coloured green from the high copper content in the subsoil (Zan means copper, skar means valley). Closer to Gulmatang, opposite the Shafat glacier, there is a fantastic view to the right of the Nun and Kun massif. Past Gulmatang the road continues through Zulichok, then past the ruins of the village of Shakar on the left; depopulated some years ago by smallpox.

Yuldo is the first town with a Zanskari population, situated six km before the Rangdum Gompa. Travellers are likely to get a friendly welcome in the small (just 10 or so houses) village. If you do not wish to continue by car to Padum or Karsha you can leave your vehicle here and take native Zanskari ponies. Prices range from Rs 25 a day and up.

The journey from here to the gompa can be shortened by cutting across the many corners along the road, especially where it runs on the northern slope of the wide, gravel plain. You have to cross a network of rivers which meander through this plain and here, as elsewhere on this trek, the river crossings are easier earlier in the day. Melting snow raises the rivers later in the day. From Yuldo the Rangdum Gompa, where 40 Gelugpa (yellow-cap) monks reside, is already visible in the distance, perched on a steep, sugarloaf mountain.

According to an inscription the monastery was built about 200 years ago by Gelek Yashy Takpa during the reign of King Tsewang Mangyal of Ladakh. As in other gompas travellers are expected to make a donation when visiting the gompa. The small mani walls, here and further along towards Padum, are more ornate than in Ladakh. Buddha reliefs are arranged on the stones and some of the stones are carved not only with the usual 'Om Mani Padme Hum' mantra but also with pictures of chortens and mandalas. There is a field suitable for camping about 1.5 km from the gompa towards the Pensi La pass. Gnats from the nearby swamp can be a nuisance but in compensation edelweiss grow in profusion.

Day 4: Rangdum Gompa-Pensi La

By vehicle you could have got to the Pensi La in one day, as noted in the introduction to this trek. It's about 25 km from the gompa to the 4401 metre Pensi La pass into Zanskar. The road runs along the north-eastern slopes, giving beautiful views of the mountains to the west. If you have come the whole way on foot and become reasonably acclimatised to the altitude, the climb to the Pensi La will be relatively easy. On your way to

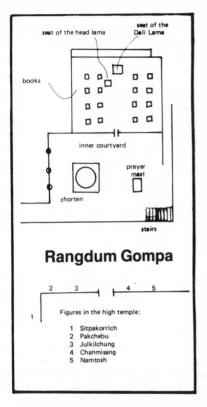

seat of the head lama

seat of the Dali Lama

books

inner courtyard

prayer mast

chorten

stairs

Rangdum Gompa

Figures in the high temple:

1 Sitpakorrlch
2 Pakchebu
3 Julkilchung
4 Chanmisang
5 Namtosh

the pass you come across stone heaps with prayer flags; travellers add their mani stones or small flags with a picture of a horse's head and the usual mantra. There are 20-odd ponds at the top of the pass where you should have no difficulty in finding a good camping place. The pass is an alpine high plain with firm, soft grass, rosemary and other alpine flowers and many red-brown marmots who pop up out of their holes to survey, warily, any intruders. The view is superb — to the south-east you can see the Takar and many other glaciers.

Several hours walk will take you to the glacier in the south-west side valley but beware of the river which, due to the melting snow, may be fordable in the morning but impossible in the afternoon. The summit at the end of the valley, of which only the peak can be seen, is 7072 metres high while the mountain to the north stands at 6873 metres. There are many unnamed peaks in the area, waiting for intrepid mountaineers to be the first to climb them.

The descent from the Pensi La into the Stod Valley is steeper than the climb up from the Rangdum Gompa, but not too difficult. The road winds about with many hairpin turns, which can be cut across on foot, to the river below. Wild rhubarb can be seen growing on the slopes. The generally used trekking route follows the road on the left bank of the Stod (or Doda). There is a bridge over the river under construction. The grass at the foot of the Pensi La furnishes a good pasturage and this is a fine camping spot, although Trakkar, shortly before the crossing of the Chinzum (Ghinzilin) is also to be recommended. Another good camping place is Chumkurmu (3920 metres).

Day 5: Pensi La-Abran

Past Chumkurmu you reach a spectacular, but short, ravine which the Chanu (Chinu) River, coming in from the left (north), has cut through a ridge. A road bridge has been built over the ravine and a temporary bridge leads down to the river and over a bridge to the other bank, up to the river terraces. The left bank route continues through Aksho (3750 metres), Chebra, crosses a tributary of the Stod and finally reaches Abran (3700 metres).

Day 6: Abran-Phé
From Abran to Phé, where there is a small and currently deserted gompa above the village, you pass the interesting little villages of Himling and Kygam, where there are only a few houses. The route is now generally heading south-east. Opposite Phé (3600 metres) the Bardur Valley opens into the broad Stod Valley. Because the Stod cannot be crossed at this point you must go further towards Padum to the Tungri Bridge, then back along the other side of the Stod, if you wish to visit the Bardur Valley with the Zongkhul Gompa or to trek over the Umasi La to Kishtwar (see Tungri-Zongkhul Gompa or Round Trip Padum-Kishtwar Trek). From Phé a route goes north-east to the Rulakung La and then north to Hanumil on the Zanskar River on the way to Padum past the Lingshot Gompa and on to Lamayuru (see Padum-Lamayuru Trek).

Day 7: Phé-Padum
The road to Padum leads through the very picturesque villages of Rantak Shuk, Shamuni and Tarkand to Tungri. A new road will probably be built from Tungri to Karsha Gompa, currently a three hour journey on foot. The footpath to Padum runs past Tungri, over the sturdy wooden bridge (stone supports) to the right-hand side of the Stod and then past Sani.

Next to Karsha the Sani (Sanee) Gompa is the most important monastery near to Padum. The gompa is unusual in that it is not built on a hill or mountain side but on flat ground and is then encircled by a stone wall in which chortens are mounted at intervals. You enter this 25-monk, red-cap monastery through a gate chorten with prayer mills. It leads to a Latho or House of God. The monastery walls are the usual symbols to ward off evil spirits and, for the same purpose, there is a goat's head filled with jewels, fortune-bringing mantras and prayer cards with 'Om Mani Padme Hum' written on them. The monastery is subject to the control of the Stagna Turku in Ladakh.

If you happen to be there at the right time, or provide a suitable donation, you may see the long ceremony in which the symbols of fortune are consecrated. The ceremony involves a goat's head being sizzled in a large pot. The value of the 'garnishings' which the monks add to the pot during the proceedings, depends upon the prosperity of the person who donated the head and for whom it is supposed to bring good fortune. Look out for the goats' heads which hang outside practically every house in Leh and other towns. In the normal course of events this symbol is renewed annually.

A small ditch, ending in a temple, leads through the gompa courtyard, it delivers enough water for the trees, a rarity in Zanskar, which grow there.

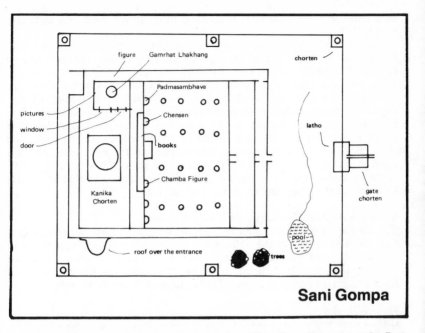

figure Gamrhat Lhakhang

chorten

Padmasambhava

pictures

window

door

Chensen

books

latho

Chamba Figure

Kanika
Chorten

gate
chorten

roof over the entrance

pool

trees

Sani Gompa

The Dukhang, with its 16 columns, houses a Chamba, a Chenren and a Padmasambhava figure amongst others. The Gonkhang is a small room behind
the altar, worth seeing for it contains an old figure of the Cho Rimpoche
and a new bookshelf lattice work for the holy writings of Kandjur. Upstairs
there are the rooms of the head lama, a storage room for tankas and, on the
left side, the room of Dorje Chan.

More interesting than these first storey rooms is the old part of the
gompa, which can be reached through the corridors which run right round
the monastery. In this low and dark passage many small Tsatsas lie on the
floor. The corridor ends in a further inner courtyard, past the large Kanika
chorten where Buddhist relics are preserved. To the right of the chorten,
squeezed between the main building of the gompa and the corridor is the
Gamshot Lhakhang in which Padmasambhava is supposed to have dwelt for
five years. A door from the inner courtyard leads into the room. If it is lock-
ed you can still look through the window and see the Padmasambhava figure
in the middle and historical scenes in half-relief on both sides. North-west,
outside the fenced in area of the gompa, there's one of the most important
cremation places in Zanskar or Ladakh — well known on account of its two
metre high dark grey boulder, on which a relief of the Maitraya has been
carved. It shines from the sacrificial oil which monks and pilgrims pour over
the Buddha image. Other smaller, crumbled away stones can be seen in the

semi-circle and the picture is completed by a prayer mast with fluttering prayer flags.

Ponies can be hired here from Rs 30 per day, porters cost Rs 10 to 25. In contrast to the ponies of the Kashmir Valley these are suitable for a trek through Karsha up the left side of the Zanskar, past the Lingshot Gompa to Lamayuru. An alternative stretch from Pensi La to Tungri leads up the right side of the Stod, at the foot of the Takar glacier, south-east through Chibre, Chukarpa, Denya and Tangar, then opposite from Phe into the Bardur Valley where the route merges, at the Zongkhul Gompa, with that described under Tungri-Zongkhul Gompa Round Trip and Padum-Kishtwar Trek. You cross the Bardur River, follow it downstream on the right bank and turn again at Ating into the Stod Valley which you then follow to Padum. This route from the Pensi La to the Tungri Bridge is shorter than that on the left bank of the Stod, but much less travelled and little known.

MANALI-PADUM TREK (by Dr Walter A Frank)
The 10 day trek from Manali to Padum can take one of two routes. One goes from Darcha over the 5100 metre Shingo La Pass to Kargiakh but to continue beyond the police post at Darcha special permission is required and this is extremely difficult to obtain. Therefore the alternative route, from Darcha over the 5345 metre Phirtse La pass, is the usual route.

Manali-Darcha
Only recently has there been a summer time bus service across the 3650 metre Rothang Pass from Manali to Keylong and on to Darcha. In Manali John Banon organises tours and vehicles for this trip. The surfaced road ends at Darcha and the gravel road which continues north-east, all the way to Leh, is suitable for four-wheel drive only and is only open to the military. From Darcha the 5100 metre Shingo La pass leads directly into the Zanskar valley but entry is restricted across the top of the pass. To trek right through the Zanskar valley to Lamayuru or Kargil will take 16 to 20 days.

ALTERNATIVE 1
Day 1: Darcha-Mane Bar (4150 metres)
Darcha, at 3300 metres, is a control post and the police chief will want to see passes. Westwards, on the bank of the Bhaga, the good road continues to the next rest place at Sarai Valley where there is a small lake (not possible to swim though) to the left of the road with a good view of the ravine. This is a good spot for an early mid-day rest. A little beyond here the road crosses to the left bank of the river by a wooden bridge, then continues to Pataiso. The river terraces broaden out to a rolling, grassy plain while the river runs in a deep ravine. Topachani will be reached late in the afternoon, fast walkers can continue to Zingzing Bar or Mane Bar.

Day 2: Mane Bar-Sarai Kilang (4460 metres)
This day's walk crosses the Baralacha La but although the route starts

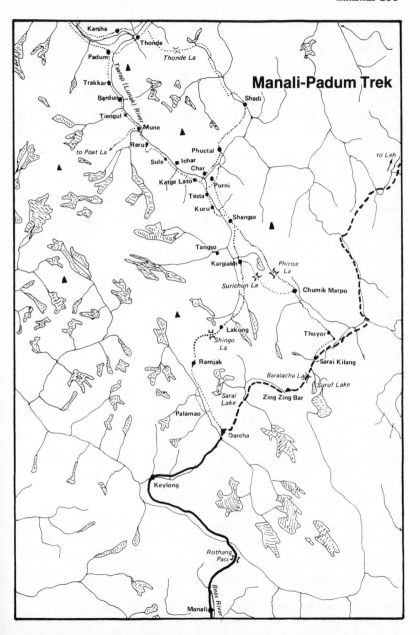

Manali-Padum Trek

almost at the pass height the climb to the top should not be underestimated. The Baralacha La is a double pass to the east and south. Even the lower, eastward pass is, at 4891 metres, higher than Mont Blanc, the highest mountain in Europe, and twice the height of Mt Kosciusko, the highest mountain in Australia! To the right the pass is close to the Suruf Lake and in good weather you can see snow-capped five and six thousand metre peaks. The southern pass is at 5100 metres and gives a view further southwards. The route continues to the left bank of the Yaman River, whose source is in the Suruf Valley, to the Sarai Kilang camping place, a grassy oasis with a brook.

Day 3: Sarai Kilang-Debni (4360 metres)
An early start is advisable, the route, now just a track, fords the river and continues until the Keylong River, entering from the left, obstructs the route. As with all river crossings the earlier you cross the lower the water level will be. Take no risks, this is a dangerous crossing. Canvas shoes should be worn for the crossing since they give more secure footing on the slippery rocks.

Further along the left bank of the Yaman there is a wide, grassy plain. If you take a short detour to the right to the edge of the river terraces there is a view of the deep Loess ravine of the Yaman, beware of the crumbling ravine edge. The route continues over the plain into the valley then gradually uphill towards the Phirtse La pass, the highest pass on the whole trek. First the 4280 metre Thoyer is reached, then the walk continues on the right bank of the Lingti Chu, following it upstream and across some deep side streams. After some more up and down walking Debni, the next overnight halt, is reached.

Day 4: Debni-Chumik Marpo (4600 metres)
Again it is wise to start early in order to cross the Kamirup, which enters the river from the left, at Kyonon. By mid-day the route climbs over a ridge to the right of the river; it's cut through by a cleft. Past here is the next river crossing; the Trukkar enters from the left from the Phirtse La Glacier. Trukkar is a rest stop but you should continue on to the overnight stop at the foot of the pass. From here a route branches off to the left over Kurziakpulo and the Surichun La to Kargiakh, but it doesn't gain much.

Day 5: Chumik Marpo-Shingsan (4460 metres)
Once again you should start early for this fine walk over the Phirtse La (5435 metres). On the pass crest there is a mini-glacier to the left and to the right a mani stone with prayer flags. Past it there is a small, rocky peak which gives a better view than the pass itself. On clear days it extends to the Karakoram range in the north. The route now descends steeply into the valley of the Phirtse Chu to the camping place in front of a rubble slope.

Day 6: Shingsan-Kargiakh (4060 metres) or Purni (3750 metres)
The rubble slope has to be climbed first thing, by noon you reach a moun-

Souvenir seller
at Lamayuru Gompa

Chomo (nun) working at
Julichen cloister near
Rizong

tain from where the Zanskar valley is visible to the west and the valley of the Kargiakh Chu to the south. The latter joins here with the Phirtse Chu at Anokh, one of the three tributaries of the Zanskar. A smaller path zig-zags steeply down to the valley. The route leads to the right into the village of Shangse, with long mani walls and a small gompa on a slope up to the right. Here the route splits, you can turn south to Kargiakh (see Alternative 2) and over the Shingo La back to Darcha, or continue north to Zanskar.

A wooden bridge crosses to the left side of the river from Shangse and you continue through the villages of Kuru, Testa and Yal before a second wooden bridge, with stone supports, leads back to the right bank. Above the bridges it is possible to camp in front of Purni. A second route also leads to Purni from Shangse keeping to the right bank all the way, but it is not so interesting because there are no villages along the way.

Day 7: Purni-Phuctal Gompa
From here the trail again follows the left bank of the Tsarap Chu, the main tributary of the Zanskar, to a swinging but stable suspension bridge — gloves are recommended when crossing. Further along the other bank a surprising view presents itself at a bend in the path — the Phuctal Gompa. The monastery is like a honeycomb, cut into a rock under a gigantic grotto, and has 70 yellow-cap monks. The library, three large and one smaller prayer rooms, the kitchens, abbot's chamber, chorten and the grave of Gangsem Sherap Sanpo, who founded Phuctal, Lekir and Rangdum, are all worth seeing. In the caves over the monastery there is a waterhole whose water level never changes; the water is said to have healing properties. There is also a stone tablet left by the Hungarian Alexander Csoma de Koros. He was one of the first explorers of Tibet and spent some time here in 1826-27.

Day 8: Phuctal Gompa-Katge Lato (3800 metres)
There is a route back along the west bank of the river to Char but it is not recommended because the Char bridge is in a dangerous condition. It is better to return along the left bank to Purni, cross the bridge and go further to the right over a ridge, past which is the Katge Lato camping place with a view over the deteriorated Char bridge, far below.

Day 9: Katge Lato-Reru (3680 metres)
There is again much variety on the day's walk. There are many picturesque villages on the bank opposite to Char — first Abnop then Dorzong, green oases in the monotonous grey-brown, and finally the Ichar castle, reached by a hanging bridge across the valley. Certain places, with rubble hills and steep, sandy slopes, call for careful treading. Three hours further walking brings you to a camping place opposite Reru, in a side valley to the left of the main route, on green grass with a brook.

Day 10: Reru-Padum (3500 metres)

From the camping place the route goes up on the plateau and over a bridge to the town of Reru with an interesting gateway chorten. The route continues past the town on the wide river terraces towards Mune. There is a gompa on a steep hill behind the town but beware of the red-cap monks' ferocious dog! From here a route leads to the left to the 6150 metres Post La pass, the highest and most difficult pass in Zanskar. It involves crossing a glacier. Continuing towards Padum you cross Tema and reach the Charmoche Kore camping ground. It goes on past Tiangul to a large rock from where the Bardun Gompa is visible. This gompa was founded by Shabdru, who also founded Hemis Gompa in Ladakh and later went to Bhutan. There are only a handful of monks working on the reconstruction of the partially ruined gompa. The climb up to the roof is worthwhile. Near the gompa there is a good camping place where a spring issues from the rocks. Two to three hours further, with the river always to the right, you will reach the wide plains of Zanskar with picturesque villages on both sides of the valley, and ahead Padum, the administrative 'capital' of Zanskar.

ALTERNATIVE 2

Although you cannot cross the Shingo La heading north from Manali to Padum, you can cross it when travelling north. It's also possible to make an eight to 10 day round trip trek from Darcha to Darcha — see Alternative 1 for details of the route from Darcha or Padum to Kargiakh. Heading south Kargiakh is the last inhabited settlement on this route until you reach Chikka, shortly before Darcha. From Kargiakh at 4060 metres you must head upstream as early as possible to the river crossing, above the point where a small stream joins it. You can camp by the mani walls or further uphill at Lakong (4450 metres). Here the valley branches out and a small valley to the right leads to the Shingo La at 5100 metres.

Day 2: Shingo La-Ramjak

The ascent to the top of the pass should be undertaken early in the morning. There is a superb view of the surrounding mountains from the crest of the pass, on which snow lies all year round. The highest peak, directly to the south, is 6797 metres. The descent from the pass follows the river on its right bank. The route to the next camping place, below the 'south peak' at a stone hut called Ramjak (4270 metres) is not difficult.

Day 3: Ramjak-Darcha

Set out early in the morning to the Barai Nallah which comes from the right and cross the Shingo La River at this point. If the snowfall in the last year has been heavy it is possible to cross by snow bridges as late as July but if the snow is melted you must wade across. The river is wild and rapid so this is probably the most difficult point of the whole trip. Continue along the left side of the high valley to a good camping place where the highest trees grow at 3700 metres. A small bridge leads there over a raging mountain brook. Another brook, with a waterfall, branches off and here you can find another camping spot. Yet another one can be found past a wooden bridge over a deep ravine. From here it is only about three hours to Darcha.

PADUM-LAMAYURU TREK
ALTERNATIVE 1 — via Zangla & Nerag
A local guide is an absolute necessity on this route.

Day 1: Padum-Thonde
As the Around Padum Trek.

Day 2: Thonde-Honia
As far as Zangla the route is the same as for the Around Padum Trek. From Zangla past Honia to Nerag is difficult, especially for horses, and should be traversed in late-summer if the previous winter had heavy snow. Rain can also make this route impassable. Above the small village of Honia there is a small spring and you should overnight here whether you have come in a one-day march from Padum or have already spent a night at Thonde along the way.

Day 3: Honia-over the Shing La-Kharmapu
The steep ascent to the Shing La pass begins after Honia. The first stretch can be dangerous due to a deep cut brook which leads directly along the steep slope. In '77 I lost my pack horse with all my personal luggage here. Past the 4500 metre high Shing La you enter a valley with tufaceous limestone formations reminiscent of those in Turkey. At Kharmapu you can camp by the river, only a few km from growing willows so that burning fuel need not be brought along. You can also camp at the foot of the double pass of Nerag La, beyond Kharmapu, but although this allows you to reach Nerag in one day the camp is at 4900 metres, just below the pass, and at this height fuel for the fire and fodder for the horses is not readily available.

Day 4: Kharmapu-foot of the Nerag La
This route is very difficult and Zanskari guides and porters are essential. At several places you have to wade across rivers and the trail crosses steep rubble hills above wild mountain brooks. Paths must be cleared (don't forget shovels) for the horses to find their footing. At one point the route leads

A   Leh, with the palace in the background and the Leh
    Gompa above it
B   Tikse Gompa
C   A visit to the tailor in Leh

through a tunnel-like rock passage in the bed of a brook and subsequently under an ice cornice, even in high summer. Even past this rough stretch the actual ascent to the pass requires some skill.

Day 5: Nerag La-Nerag

The view from the Nerag La, over the village 1500 metres below and to the mountain range on the other side of the Zanskar, is superb. Shortly before Nerag you can again find burnable wood and there are some suitable camping spots above the village. Pasturage for the horses and fresh water are also on hand.

Day 6: Nerag-Yulching-Singi La-Photosar

Two km below Nerag there is a wooden bridge across the Zanskar which is suitable for horses. Immediately on the other side of the Zanskar (3400 metres), which here flows in eastwards in a deep-cut bed towards Nimmu, the ascent towards the Singi La begins. The first saddle is at 3990 metres, the second at 3930 metres. Near Yulching the route bends left to the Lingshot Gompa (see Padum-Lamayuru Trek, Alternative 2).

At Yulching one can marvel at the irrigation techniques of the Zanskaris, above the village melted ice-water from the mountain brooks is first collected in ponds and warmed through insulation then conducted into the struggling small fields with their poor soil. There is a grand panorama to the east with waterfalls cascading down the rock walls on the other side of the Singi La or 'Lion Pass' (4850 metres). The trekking path wanders around the western valley slope through many side valleys. Mountain wanderers can take a short cut on the northern rubble slopes by cutting across the serpentine curves on the route leading to the valley. The valley floor is quite marshy due to the brook flowing eastwards from Photosar into the Photang River. In summer it is richly grown and provides good grazing pasturage. The route leaves the western side of the valley and crosses a small pass then through a mountain ridge between the valley it came out of and the Photang Valley in which lies Photosar. If you arrive late do not go straight into the village but camp on the southern slope of the Photang River, opposite Photosar, where there is also pasturage for horses.

Day 7: Photosar-Shirshi La-Hanuputta

According to our Zanskari guide Photosar means 'salt-cave'. It stands at 4100 metres on a small plateau on the other side of the eastward flowing Photang River. The name touches on the fact that during the rain, so much

A Wall-painting in Tikse Gompa
B Tanka in Lamayuru Gompa
C Ladakhi man spinning yarn

salt is washed out of the rockwall past Photosar that the fields around the village slowly become infertile due to this mineralised irrigation. Sited 50 metres above the river Photosar is an attractive place even when the peace is disturbed by loudspeakers, playing music from All India Radio. Upstream from Photosar, to the west, is the bridge over the Photang River.

The route to Lamayuru follows the Photang-Drogpo to the west, first on the southern banks then, after three km, on the northern. The route leads through terraced fields then turns north-east into a side valley of the Photang River. En route to the pass you can see marmots and rock ptarmigans. It's only a short trek to the Shirshi La (or Sirsir La) and only the last hundred metres is steep and strenuous. Above the top of the pass you find, as on every pass in Ladakh and Zanskar, a Latho ('Godhouse') with coloured prayer flags and mani stones. The flags show the head of a horse in the middle and every Buddhist traveller will leave behind a flag with a mantra printed on it. Do not collect these as souvenirs under any circumstances! The descent from the pass into the valley of the Tang is steep but not very difficult. From here there are two routes to Lamayuru:

via Hanupatta and Wanla
through the valley of the Shillakong to Wanla

The route via Hanuputta descends from the Shirshi La through the valley of the Tang on the right river bank, high on the slope to the north-east. After some kilometres it crosses a bridge to the left bank where the river is wider and the path better. As in most Zanskari villages it is difficult to obtain food supplies in Hanuputta.

Day 8: Hanuputta-Wanla-Shilla-Prikiti La-Lamayuru

The route from Hanuputta to Wanla is difficult and not always passable — especially for pack animals. Past Hanuputta the route leads down to the river and forces through a narrow spot to where you can ford the river. A little later it climbs above the river to a place where it cuts deeply through the rock. At times the path ends at the water and you must continue along the bank to find a place shallow enough to cross to the other side. The path then winds steeply up the rocks where the ponies clamber like deer. Heading north-west there are dangerous stretches where the ponies must be unloaded and led across step-by-step. The process repeats itself for a couple of hours — unload, lead the ponies across, carry the loads across, load the ponies, continue on. Finally the mountains open and the path becomes much more hospitable.

The next village offers the inviting shade of apricot trees and the route then leads along a precipice and descends to the bottom of the valley. Here one goes past field after field and large settlements until Wanla is reached. A left turn takes you into the Shillakong Valley and shortly past the village of Shilla you turn right (north). Early in the morning a part of the route in the narrow, barren valley to the 3900 metre Prikita La ('Lizard Pass') is still in shadow — for both man and beast this is very pleasant. By noon the climb in the strong sun can become an ordeal. From the Prikiti La the route leads north-east into the Lamayuru Valley then, once the cultivated fields have been reached, a short way to the west.

The Lamayuru Monastery is first seen to the right on a sugarloaf mountain. The trail leads westwards from the monastery hill through the village of Lamayuru to the Fatu La-Nimmu-Leh road, on which from the Prikiti La you can already see trucks crawling. Careful — Zanskari horses are not accustomed to traffic and scare easily, the noise of movie cameras can also frighten them! You should unload them as quickly as possible on the road. From here you can take a bus or truck to Leh or to Kargil and Srinagar.

Alternative Route — final day
Day 7 to 9: Photosar-Shirshi La-over the Tang River-Niuche La-into the Shillong Valley-Shilla-Prikiti La-Lamayuru

If the Hanuputta-Wanla Route is impassable then this route may be an alternative. It crosses the Tang River (4500 metres) past the Shirshi La whereas the Hanuputta route follows this river. Cross the river as early as possible in the morning since the river is very rapid after mid-day. The trail then goes north-west into the side valley opposite. If you get here in the afternoon you should seek a camping spot with pasturage for the horses. The last kilometres to the 5050 metre Niuche La are barren and terrible for camping. On the other side of the pass, to the north-west there is another camping possibility at 4450 metres. The route continues down into the Shillakong river-valley which it follows to Shilla. This 20 to 25 km route is unique since the valley is so narrow that at times you have to go along the riverbed! Note the mineral layers in this ravine, indicative of the dislocation the creation of the mountain range must have caused. Shortly before Shilla there are three unstable wooden bridges, one of which is particularly bad. The route crosses a stone bridge with a Latho to a warm spring which is said to have healing properties. From the top of the pass you can reach Shilla (3300 metres) in one day, from where the route is the same as the Hanuputta-Wanla alternative.

ALTERNATIVE 2 — via Lingshot Gompa
Day 1: Padum-Pishu

You can go via Rubruk to Yalong (Yulung) and Karsha or via Sani, the Tungri Bridge and then downstream along the Stod which is altogether a six hour trek to Karsha. From Karsha you continue on the left bank of the Zanskar to where the Stod joins with the Tsarap Lingti Chu and through Ridam to Pishu. Pishu is six hours from Karsha. There are camping spots with grass for the pack animals by the river. Past Karsha the fields stop and the relatively infrequently travelled path is bordered by sandstone. The mountains creep closer to the trail, constant erosion has carved them into fantastic shapes. The geological layers are quite easy to observe. Before the village of Pishu the banks get narrower and narrower and at Pishu you can cross the river by a rope bridge, as related in the Around Padum Trek.

Day 2, 3 &4: Pishu-Lingshot Gompa

Past Pishu the route leads at first along the bank of the Zanskar until the village of Pigmo (Pigmu or Pittu) is reached after four to five hours. Some tributaries of the Zanskar must be crossed but they should present no problem. The path then runs very close to a brook, so close that you can bargain on getting wet feet at some stage. You can stay overnight near the small village of Hunamul (Hanomul) past where the route runs through grassland. A route branches off to the left towards Rulakung and over the Rulakung La to Phé (see Kargil-Padum Trek). The valley narrows, the path is hewn through rocks, the bank is steep and at one point, which the rocks overhang, ponies can only be led unloaded. Once past this difficult point a short climb leads over a rubble hill while to the right the Zanskar storms past the practically vertical bank. The trail continues along the steep slopes, over which the native ponies go with great certainty. After a few hours the path leads left to a small pass which is indicated on some maps as the Purfi La. The pass is only steep over the last hundred metres. On the north side the trail makes tight bends through grass slopes and bushes then turns right and continues over broken rocks and rubble. At a sharp bend the river and a ruined bridge can be seen far below.

With a mountain rope and poplars, which grow on the bank, you can build a makeshift bridge at a narrow point. The pack animals can, unloaded, swim the river at a wider, less rapid point. On the other side the climb begins to a small pass and at this height the trail leads along a steep canyon wall then slowly gets easier. There is grass and a good camping spot in the valley below.

Continuing upstream towards Lingshot there are snow bridges which can still be crossed in mid-summer. After a while the valley widens and the horses have no more strenuous climbing. The path then turns right and soon the pass saddle is visible with the usual mani stones and prayer flags. From the top of the Hamalun La (or Hanuma La) there is a fine view of the Lingshot Gompa on the other side of the valley. The descent, over sand hills, is steep and several hills and rises must be crossed during the descent into the valley. After a few hours the village of Lingshot and the Lingshot Gompa are reached. Lingshot (also Lingshed) has 60 monks and is famous, in Zanskar, for its school of painting. In the gompa there are a large number of superb paintings made with bright mineral pigments.

Day 5: Lingshot-Yulchung

Past Lingshot the route leads eastwards over mountains and passes to Yulchung. Turning right here will take you back to the Zanskar Valley via Nerag.

a Zanskari in Padum

Day 6, 7 & 8: Yulchung-Lamayuru
The last three days are as Alternative 1 for the Padum-Lamayuru Trek.

PADUM-KISHTWAR TREK (by Kurt & Ingrid Zehetner)
This trek from Padum, passing over the 5234 metre high Umasi La, can only be undertaken with local porters. Since most of the porters do not understand any English it is worth discussing the route with the porters before departure, the Tourist Officer will interpret. One porter per person is recommended. Zanskari porters are faster, harder-working and generally friendlier than Kashmiri pony-drivers so there will undoubtedly be many more trekkers using Zanskaris in the future. The price is about Rs 20 per day for a porter. They will only set out for the Umasi La in good, fog-free, weather so you should also allow Rs 10 per day for waiting time. No great difficulties are experienced on this trek so long as you are fit, healthy and acclimatised to the altitude. The ascent to the Umasi La pass is steeper but shorter from the Padum side than the Kishtwar side. Leggings are recommended because of the snow on the Umasi La and it is also wise to have a waterproof tent. Bring food supplies from Padum although you can also get some food in Matsel and Atholi.

Day 1: Padum-Ating
Do not hire horses, which are inappropriate for this trek, see the Tourist Officer for porters. It's a pleasant march to Ating with a bridgeless glacier river to cross — the earlier in the day the better.

Day 2: Ating-shortly before Ratrat
You turn from the Stod Valley into the south-west side valley of the Bardur and arrive at the Zongkhul Gompa. The foundations of this monastery is attributed to the abbot Naropa, whose ceremonial dagger in the rocks of Zongkhul attracts many pilgrims today. The monastery belongs to the redcap sect and had 20 monks about 15 to 20 years ago; today one seldom sees more than two or three. The route from Ating leads directly to the monastery in about two or three hours along a meandering path.

The monastery is built directly on a rock wall surrounded by about 10 stone houses which, from a distance, blend in to the grey background. Like the Hemis Gompa in Ladakh, the Zongkhul Gompa has an 'eagle's nest' which can be reached in about 10 minutes from the gompa — which offers superb views from the roof terrace. It's an easy seven hour climb to the excellent Ganra rest place which also has a wonderful view.

Day 3: Umasi La-shortly before Bhuswas
A 5½ hour climb takes you over a glacier and a snowfield to the top of the pass with its remarkable crest. On the other side of the somewhat easier descent you go through snowfields and then across another glacier. The walk to the camping spot, about an hour before Bhuswas, is about 12 hours. There is a spring, a river and grass at the site.

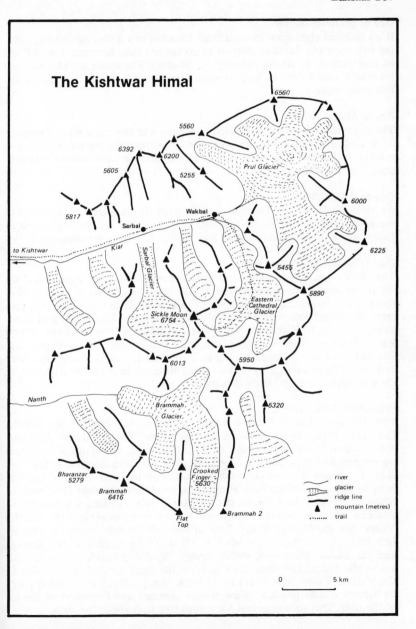

The Kishtwar Himal

6560

5560
6392
6200
5605
5255
5817

Wakbal
Sarbal
Prul Glacier
6000

to Kishtwar
Kiar
6225

Sarbal Glacier
5455
5890

Eastern
Cathedral
Glacier

Sickle Moon
6754

6013
5950

Nanth

Brammah
Glacier
5320

Bharanzar
5279

Brammah
6416

Crooked
Finger
5630

Flat
Top

Brammah 2

0   5 km

river
glacier
ridge line
mountain (metres)
trail

Day 4: Bhuswas-Matsel

It's a pleasant eight-hour descent from Bhuswas to a police station but nothing will persuade Zanskari porters to go further than here and it is difficult to hire porters in Matsel (Machail or Machel). For about Rs 150 you can eventually hire a donkey to Kishtwar. Prices on this side of the pass are significantly higher.

Day 5: Matsel-Atholi

The river valley becomes increasingly narrow and the route more strenuous as it leads over an unbroken sequence of ascents and descents. Atholi is reached in the late afternoon and the police station commandant is hospitable. Beware of the gnats!

Day 6: Atholi-Shasho

As on the previous day the route is hard work. It takes six to eight hours to reach the Shasho rest place, a small, dirty, uncared for site with three or four huts on the mountain side. A stay in the huts is not recommended.

Day 7: Shasho-Galar-Kishtwar

The route continues to climb and drop and continues to be strenuous. During the monsoon it can be marshy and seem endless. Galar is reached after about seven hours and a road leads from here to Kishtwar. Work is in progress to extend this road from Galar back towards Atholi. Two or three buses go daily to Kishtwar from Galar, a distance of about 30 km. If you leave Atholi very early and travel fairly fast you can get to Galar in one day. The last bus leaves Galar about 5 pm, if you miss it you must overnight here and go to Kishtwar the next day. Long distance buses leave Kishtwar at about 6 am for Srinagar and other places.

PADUM-NIMMU TREK

The first section of this trek as far as Hanuputta is covered in the Padum-Lamayuru Trek reports. Between Hanuputta and Wanla you turn right into a side valley, north of the Zanskar mountain chain, and continue upstream over a pass and then down a brook which is a western side arm of the Zanskar. You reach the Zanskar a few km to the north of the village of Chiling, with its chorten of Guru Padmasambhava, and follow the river's left bank to Nimmu. A rope bridge crosses the Zanskar between Chiling and Nimmu so you can turn at Sumdo (the village where three rivers meet) into the Markha Valley. See the Markha Valley Trek in the Ladakh section and the Padum-Leh Trek. Near Nimmu, towards Leh and above the junction of the Zanskar and the Indus, there is a sturdy bridge capable of taking pack animals across the Indus. The route then goes on the right bank of the Zanskar to the Markha Valley. The direct route from Nerag through the Zanskar gorge to Nimmu is only possible in the winter (January and February) on the ice of the river. This strenuous and hazardous trek lasts about five days.

PADUM-LEH — Markha Valley Trek (by Walter Kamm)
This hard but very rewarding trek takes you from Padum to Zangla as on the Padum-Lamayuru Trek. At Zangla you turn right to the Charcha La Pass (5200 metres) and from there to Tilta Sumdo via Tom To. Here a path turns left towards Nimmu but you must turn right then in 12 to 15 km turn left towards Kurna Sumdo. To the right it goes further via Lapurbo to Kurna. Kurna Sumdo the route continues past Ruberung and the Ruberung La pass (5000 metres) to the Markha Gompa in another day or two.

Here the route diverges: one route goes from the gompa to the right, past Hankar and in two days reaches Chogdo after which comes Hemis and finally along the Indus to Leh. The other route turns left from the Markha Gompa past Skiu, the Ganda La (or Kanda La) pass at 4800 metres and on to Rumbagh. From Rumbagh it crosses the 4880 metre Namlung Pass and on to Leh. This route is only recommended for the second half of August because many crossings have to be made over large rivers. Often the water is chest high and by September it is once again too cold.

PADUM
The locals say Padum, foreigners generally Padam. The capital of Zanskar, it stands on the southern part of a wide, fertile plain in which the Tsarap Lingti Chu (Lunak River) and the Stod (Doda) River join to form the Zanskar (Cham) River. There are only about a hundred houses in Padum, built on a barren, rock-covered hill. New houses are built in a semi-circle in the fields. The small hill, on which a fort once stood, today has only a small, insignificant gompa with its entrance facing the river. The chapel is practically empty apart from some recently painted murals.

Unlike most other Zanskaris, who are practically all Buddhists, about 300 of Padum's 700 inhabitants are not Ladakhis but Indo-Aryans like the Baltis and Lahulis and are followers of the Sunnite Moslem sect. The division into these two completely different population groups is instantly recognisable by the clothing they wear. The people are very hospitable but also shy, in the first four years after the re-opening of Zanskar to foreign visitors only a couple of hundred people passed through. Making contact with the children will result in an invitation into a house. If you wish to make a longer trek the Administration or the Tourist Bureau (yes!) will be happy to answer any questions and are very helpful with the hiring of horses (there are about 40 in Padum) or obtaining accommodation. An overnight stay in a private house in Padum will cost Rs 10 to Rs 20 per person.

There are a few shops in Padum, like Mohd Amid's, but only the basics are available and prices are high. The government buildings outside Padum include a morse radio station which, when necessary, can call for a military helicopter from Leh, which can land near the Karsha Gompa on the other side of the Stod River. The local water is milky-white and highly mineralised and even when boiled for tea is not very palatable. In July and August stray monsoon clouds sometimes creep into Zanskar from the plains of India and

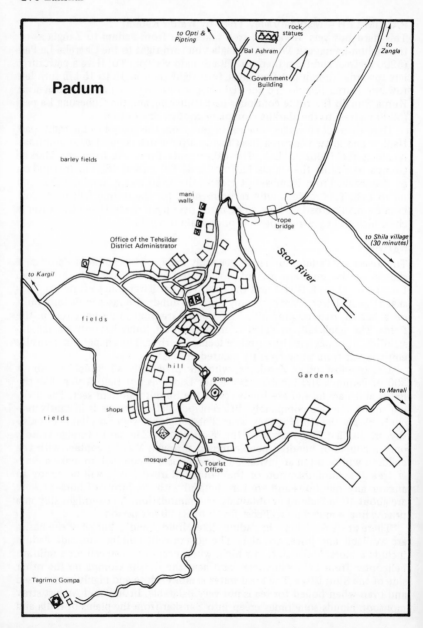

to Opti & Pipting

rock statues

to Zangla

Bal Ashram

Government Building

Padum

barley fields

mani walls

Office of the Tehsildar District Administrator

rope bridge

to Shila village (30 minutes)

to Kargil

Stod River

fields

hill

gompa

Gardens

to Manali

shops

fields

mosque

Tourist Office

Tagrimo Gompa

heavy showers are not uncommon in the afternoon. Therefore the excursion to Karsha should be made in the morning.

West of Padum, a good half hour's climb, is the small Tagrimo Gompa with an interesting Dukhang with a stamped clay floor. The paintings on the side walls are, unlike most gompas, not directly on the wall but on tanka cloths.

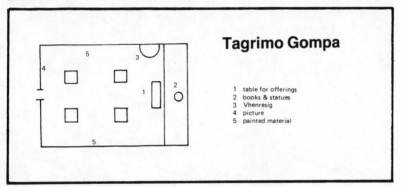

Tagrimo Gompa

1 table for offerings
2 books & statues
3 Vhenresig
4 picture
5 painted material

PADUM-THONDE-ZANGLA-KARSHA GOMPA-PADUM ROUNDTRIP
Day 1: Padum-Thonde

From Padum the route leads over the eastern rope bridge, below the town on the right bank of the Lunak, one of the source rivers of the Zanskar. Kashmiri porters are unwilling to transport loads over these rope bridges. Zanskaris are the true specialists and the performance of 'oncoming traffic' can be acrobatic! The route to Thonde follows the river, at a distance above the rubble plain through which the river has carved its path. Thonde (also spelt Stongday or Stongde) is a river oasis with a monastery enthroned above it, you take the direct route to Zangla, which follows the Zanskar River. it's a five to six hour walk from Padum.

Thonde is an important town for trekking tours towards Lamayuru because this is the first place where horses can be hired on this side of the rope bridge. They should be ordered from Padum so that they are already waiting when you get to Thonde. The best view of the irrigated fields, in which the semi-circle of houses lie, is from the monastery. It's a strenuous ascent, particularly in the heat of mid-day, but one should not fail to see this monastery which shows to visitors, at least at the moment, the intact life of a monastic society.

At mid-day you can see the feeding of the monastery school pupils — everyone receives tsampa balls to eat. You may be lucky enough to view the ritual purification of various ceremonial objects or you may see the manufacture of butter candles. Descending from the monastery you can see, to the left of the mountains on either side of the Zanskar River, the distant form of Karsha Gompa. A difficult, dangerous and not to be recommended

one of Zanskar's many terrifying suspension bridges

route turns eastward from Thonde through the Shadi Ravine to the Phuctal Gorge — see the Padum-Phuctal report.

Day 2: Thonde-Zangla

The route to Zangla follows the Zanskar River further to the north-east. Zozar (Zazar or Tsazar) is the next large town and after this the picturesque trail continues partly on the banks of the Zanskar, which makes it impassable at high water. Half way between Zozar and Zangla a rope bridge leads across the Zanskar.

Zangla does not have much to offer apart from the rebuilt 'castle' of the one-time kings of Zanskar. Here you will see more newly built chortens than elsewhere in Zanskar, a sign of the living nature of Buddhism in this area. The son of the king, once a monk and an important tanka painter, now wears a nylon wind jacket and sunglasses and spends several months of each year in Delhi. Times are changing. If you should be invited in for a cup of butter tea (or 'sweet' tea) try to have a look at the 'palace' Dukhang. Some of the tankas in this room were painted by the king's son.

The remains of the old and decayed fortifications of the king lie on the mountains above the village. The prince of Zangla compared the site of these ruins to the head of an eagle but they did not impress us enough to want to climb the hill! We did enjoy making friends with the children during our stay with the royal family.

Day 3: Zangla-Karsha Gompa

In Zangla the Markha trek turns towards Leh (see Padum-Leh Trek) but if you wish to go to Lamayuru it is best to follow the Zanskar River further along to Honia (see the Padum-Lamayuru Trek). To return from Zangla, crossing over the river to Karsha en route to Padum, you must go some km back towards Zozar and cross the Zanskar by a scenic rope bridge. The route branches right past the rope bridge and continues past Pishu and the Lingshot Gompa towards Lamayuru (see Padum-Lamayuru) or left towards Padum. Five to six hours ascending walk to the south-west takes you past Rinam towards Yalong and the Karsha Gompa. A direct route also leads to this gompa from Padum and over the river terrace plains to the north towards Yalong. Yalong is on the other bank of the Stod, one of the source rivers of the Zanskar, below the Karsha Gompa.

Karsha is the largest and most important monastery in Zanskar, has more than 150 yellow-cap monks and is subject to the control of the younger brother of the Dalai Lama. The white-washed walls of the houses and chapels of the gompa, which perches like a falcon's nest on the rocks above the Stod/Zanskar Rivers, can be seen from a great distance away. A sweat-raising climb is eventually rewarded by superb panoramic views over the valley. The chapel of the monastery, which contains a further three prayer rooms, has places for 35 lamas. Behind the seat of the Dalai Lama's brother there is a figure of Lhaso Cho Rimpoche with a golden crown inset with

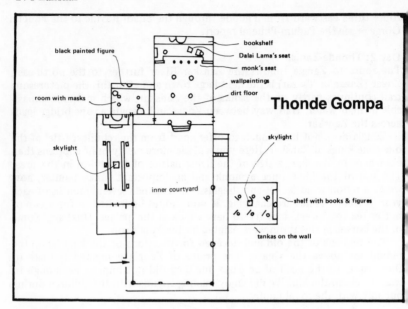

carnelian and turquoise gemstones. It was brought here from Lhasa in the early '60s but the three small windows let in little light to the room so it is difficult to see clearly. Karsha's most important festival is the Karsha Gostor with Cham mask dances on the 26th to 29th day of the 11th month of the Tibetan calendar — usually early January. The library of the gompa is also worth seeing and Karsha's butter tea is widely renowned.

Day 4: Karsha-Padum
You can cross the Stod by a rubber dinghy (cost is Rs 5) left behind in '76 by a German party or you can take the route over Lami and Kusser towards Rankiut where you can stay overnight although Tungri is better. A sturdy

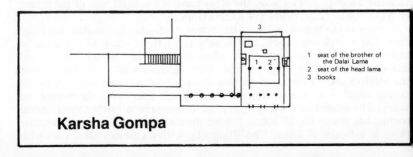

wooden bridge (the Tungri Bridge) crosses the Stod and the route then follows the river westward (upstream) to Turkun (3550 metres). There is a small, but interesting, gompa with nuns above picturesque Tungri. From Tungri the route leads back past the Sani Gompa, Salapi and Ranzam to Padum.

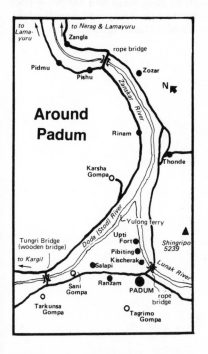

TREKS AROUND PADUM
There are a number of round trips that can be made from Padum but in any event a day's excursion to the old residence of the King of Zanskar is well worthwhile. In 1976 the small castle, Gyalpoy Pothang, was in a dreadful state of repair and totally uninhabitable due to the effects of rain and avalanches. Since then it has been rebuilt with much local help. The old king, whose uncle belongs to the Spitok Gompa in Ladakh, is still alive and his son represents Zanskar in the Indian parliament.

TUNGRI-ZONGKHUL GOMPA ROUNDTRIP
(by Dr Walter A Frank)
From Padum you follow the Stod River to the Sani and then leave the Stod Valley and follow the Sani southwards towards the Muni La pass. About halfway to the pass crest you turn west into a side valley, cross a saddle and arrive at the Huttra camping place below the Umasi La. The trail leads downstream by the Bardur to the Ganra camping place near the Zongkhul Gompa (see Padum-Kishtwar Trek) and then back to the Stod Valley. At Chibra Stod you head downstream to the east via Ating, Drokund, Shagur, Murkum and Turkum to Tungri. The trip takes about four days.

PADUM-PHUCTAL GOMPA — by the Shadi Gorge (by Walter Kamm)
This four or five day trek can be extremely dangerous and difficult although it might, superficially, seem like an attractive way of making a round trip Padum-Phuctal-Padum. The route from Padum runs to Thonde then eastwards (to the right) into the mountains and across the 5492 metre Thonde

La. To the top of the pass the route is quite easy but from there it's hell through the gorges. Because the route has not been regularly travelled for years the path has deteriorated and much dangerous clambering plus river and mountain crossing is necessary. Horses are unusable! There is only one tiny village, Shadi, on the whole route and even that is in a side valley. Many stretches are dangerous due to the vertical rock walls and the loose rock slopes high above the turbulent rivers winding their way far below the trail. From Phuctal you soon rejoin the usual Padum-Manali route.